**To Be or Not To Be Happy: Perspectives on Well-being**

**To Be or Not To Be Happy: Perspectives on Well-being**

Written by: Austin Mardon, Thomas Banks, Madeline Langier, Rob Mcweeny, and Jonathan Weibe

Edited by: Alyssa Kulchisky

Designed by: Josh Kramer

Published by Golden Meteorite Press
2021

*To Be or Not To Be Happy: Perspectives on Well-being*
Copyright © 2021 by Austin Mardon
All rights reserved.

This book or any portion thereof may not be reproduced or used in any manner whatsoever without the express written permission of the publisher except for the use of brief quotations in a review.

First Printing: 2021

ISBN: 978-1-77369-650-8

Golden Meteorite Press
103 11919 82 St NW
Edmonton, AB T5B 2W3
www.goldenmeteoritepress.com
aamardon@yahoo.ca
Alberta, Canada

# Table of Contents

Chapter 1: Theorizing Happiness ........................................................... 1
Chapter 2: Western Perspectives on Happiness ............................. 21
Chapter 3: Eastern Perspectives on Happiness .............................. 35
Chapter 4: The Similarities and Differences between Perspectives ................................................................................................................ 55
Chapter 5: The Science of Subjective Well-being ......................... 69
Chapter 6: Sociology of Well-being ..................................................... 77
Chapter 7: Economics of Happiness .................................................. 87
Chapter 8: Social-Scientific Perspectives to Happiness & Positive Psychology ...................................................................................... 97
Chapter 9: Becoming Happier - From Theory to Practice .......... 113
References ................................................................................................. 127

# Chapter 1: Theorizing Happiness

*"The important question is not, what will yield to man a few scattered pleasures, but what will render his life happy on the whole amount."*
— Joseph Addison

Happiness, like feelings of fear and sorrow among other primal conditions of life, has long been of interest to philosophers. According to the literature concerning the philosophy of happiness, philosophers have defined happiness as either a state of mind possessed by an individual or a life that goes well for individuals living it (Haybron, 2020). Let us briefly address these views with greater specificity. For some philosophers, happiness can be defined simply as a positive emotional condition that exists as an individual's state of mind. Philosophers assessing this theory of happiness have also investigated the extent to which this positive state of mind is valuable (in essence whether a meaningful life involves pursuing it). Another variety of philosophers conceive of happiness as well-being (in essence a life that goes well). This philosophical view of happiness is obviously bound up in perception and subjectivity as what is in the best interest of an individual may not be objectively definable. The purpose of this chapter is to address these different philosophical conceptions of happiness and investigate if it is reasonable to accept them as our preferred views of happiness.

## Happiness as Pleasure

Epicurus was a Greek philosopher living in ancient Athens. He founded a teaching school known as the Garden to compete with Plato's Academy and Aristotle's Lyceum. In his work, Epicurus devised a philosophy of happiness centered around the subjective experience of pleasure and pain. According to Epicurus, "Pleasure is the first good. It is the beginning of every choice and every aversion. It is the absence of pain in the body and of troubles in the soul." (Hicks, 2004). In other words, Epicurus set out the view that the kinds of actions that are good and worthwhile are those actions that bring about pleasure and minimise pain. Epicurus may point to childlike or animalistic instincts as evidence for pleasure and pain as foundational to sensible behavior. Indeed, from a modern scientific theory of evolution, pain and pleasure could be regarded as useful internalised positive or negative reinforcements for influencing behavior that increased or decreased one's likelihood of reproduction and survival (Damasio & Carvalho, 2013). Epicurus's view about living life according to pleasure maximisation rings true in the modern age where consumption and production are oriented around often fleeting pleasures. Therefore, as our first philosophy of happiness, it is a fruitful line of inquiry to investigate Epicureanism further as it could be considered fundamental to the development of modern conceptions of the good-life as a life of pleasure.

According to Epicurus, the role of philosophy is to be useful in that it must produce rules or maxims that individuals can adopt and follow to achieve happiness. To be clear, Epicurus did not regard all forms of pleasure as equality worthwhile to pursue. He devised several categories for pleasure. First,

Epicurus defined those pleasures that are natural and necessary for life (ie. impossible to eliminate and easy to satisfy such as hunger and thirst). Second, Epicurus defined those pleasures that are natural and unnecessary for life (ie. possible to eliminate and harder to satisfy such as comfort). Third, Epicurus defined certain pleasures as unnatural and unnecessary (ie. wealth, power, fame). For Epicurus, unnatural and unnecessary pleasures are dangerous because they are insatiable demands and are artificial products only of society and socialisation. Based on his theory, Epicurus would prefer a modest life wherein his natural and necessary pleasures could be readily satisfied and he was unattached or afraid of losing access to any other form of pleasure such as those which are natural yet unnecessary for life. Overall, it would be apt to say that Epicurus had a minimalist view on pleasure maximisation.

Epicureanism set the stage for more philosophically complex theories of happiness as pleasure devised by 19th century philosophers Jeremy Bentham and John Stuart Mill. These philosophers devised a philosophy of pleasure and happiness known as utilitarianism. Similar to epicureanism, utilitarianism suggested that right actions are those that maximise pleasure and minimise pain. For philosophers of this school of happiness, it is clear happiness is the ground of all action. They would argue that questioning the intention of a given behavior all the way down to its basic principles until you one cannot ask 'why' anymore appears always to lead back into the pursuit of happiness at a basic level. The focus of utilitarianism was also a scientific approach to understanding pleasure as happiness. Mill accepted, like Bentham, that "all desirable things [...] are desirable either for the pleasure inherent in themselves, or as means to the promotion of pleasure and the prevention of pain" but thought some types of experiences, namely those that are intellectual, were more meaningful than others (Mill, 1861, p. 10).

Bentham is best known for the creation of a happiness algorithm (which individuals can use in their daily life to supposedly best guide their behaviour) which functions to assess the total amount of pleasure an action is likely to produce and, therefore, whether an action is worthwhile. Bentham's algorithm for assessing a potential action based on its tendency to produce pleasure included several variables. In particular, he thought one should consider pleasure intensity (relative strength of sensation), duration (length in chronological time), certainty (whether it's likely an action will produce pleasure), remoteness (whether an action will produce pleasure now or in the future), fecundity (whether the action will have a pleasure snowball effect), and purity (whether having the pleasure now will come with pain later).

While this algorithm appears complex when presented in this manner, many people make these sorts of rational calculations in a less structured manner when deciding how to act, such as saving for the future in retirement or constraining their intake of alcohol to an optimal point without causing a hangover. These conceptions of happiness as pleasure as devised by Epicurus, Mill, and Bentham are part of a richer theory of ethics, the content of which is not directly relevant for the purposes of this chapter. It suffices to say for our purposes that these theories translate roughly into a theory of happiness known as hedonism, a belief that pleasure is the only thing that is intrinsically good.

## Universalised Happiness

To be clear, hedonism is a philosophy of happiness that identifies the experience of pleasure as an activity which is intrinsically good on its own account, not for any other purpose. In contradistinction, hedonism would argue that money or technological achievement are instrumentally good because they enable individuals to access goods and services that have a tendency to produce happiness. These theories of happiness as pleasure-maximising are perhaps best tested in thought experiments to understand if they hold water. For instance, we could devise a thought experiment to see whether it is truly desirable to live a life of absolute pleasure. Imagine you could healthily reside for the rest of your life inside a sensory deprivation chamber hooked up to a machine which produced in your brain only one sensation: intense ecstatic pleasure. Is this a life you would voluntarily choose to live? The pure pleasure maximising utilitarians and hedonists would think this life is ideal. However, I suspect that most readers would consider something to be missing in this life and would therefore opt-out of a life defined by pure pleasure. This experiment, if we are to accept these presumptive conclusions, provides a strong indication that happiness consists less in subjective pleasure as a state of mind and more in subjective experience. Happiness is an activity and process of being and not merely a state of mind.

This idea of happiness as an activity is not new. For context, Aristotle was perhaps the earliest philosopher that viewed happiness as an activity. As we covered in depth in the previous chapter, Aristotle believed that the final end of humanity is happiness not as a state but as an activity, known as eudaimonia (a condition of flourishing and living well) and that the goal of an individual should be leading a successful human life. Aristotle's conception of happiness fits into a much more complex view of ethics and metaphysics (in essence the philosophy that deals with abstract grounds of knowledge) which for present purposes is best left unaddressed. For now, we may simply recognize the history of this view of happiness and devise another thought experiment for testing whether a conception of happiness as a product of experience is ideal.

In building off the last thought experiment, is it possible to imagine a more sophisticated machine that could allow users to simulate any reality or experience imaginable to the extent that it is indistinguishable from the known world (Nozick, 2014). We may refer to this as an experience or dream machine. If we are to assess the question of whether happiness consists in the activity of experience, we must ask: would it be an ideally happy life to enter this machine if you knew doing so would preclude you from ever returning to the world as you know it? For some, the proposal of entering the dream machine would be problematic as it would be to an extent 'fake' reality and a version of death in the real world. However, on the other hand, the dream machine would be a paradise where you could experience any reality. Think of how it would feel to have the capability to 'live' authentically any experience ever had by any object, animal, or person since the beginning of recorded time to the farthest reaches of the theorised future. Think of how it would feel to have an almost infinite capacity to imagine different existances based on the history of the world and your own creative power. Think of how it would feel to have the capability to temporarily forget you were inside the experience machine at all and then 'wake up' when a particular experience ended.

We suggest it would be foolish to decline to step into the machine when the likely alternative would be an otherwise predictable life-span and life-course in the known world.

We also suggest that the dream-machine thought experiment indicates that happiness resides in the fulfilment of desire. We conclude, therefore, that what is intrinsically good for an individual is to realise the fulfillment of their intrinsic desires. Let us briefly discuss this philosophy of happiness in a greater degree of detail. This view of happiness as the fulfilment of desire requires tuning to work. For example, it is impossible to conclude that an individual could benefit from the fulfillment of desires which they had at a particular point in time but did not know were fulfilled (Bruckner, 2016). This clear truth indicates that a theory of happiness must concern one's own perspective and the information of which they are aware: the fulfillment or non-fulfillment of the intrinsic desire one has about one's own life.

Even with this tuning, there are still challenges with this view of happiness. A theory of happiness, for instance, needs to recognise that an individual could gain happiness from events that are beyond the fulfillment of desires they have presently or could reasonably have within the course of their life. This would be the case of a life-long prisoner whose life in confinement was constrained to a small concrete compound with no view to the outside world. This individual may have their desires fulfilled from time to time, but their scope of knowledge about what desires there are to be fulfilled is so limited that we could not say they were living an ideally happy life. This clear truth indicates that there are some foundational aspects to happiness that are built into life and are good whether or not we know of them.

These foundational aspects of happiness could reasonably be collected and put into a list of things that are objectively good. Therefore, the most reasonable theory of happiness would be a List Theory of Objective Value, which we will develop in what follows. This theory centres on the belief that happiness consists in the fulfillment of desires and the capacity to realise a broad set of desires about particular aspects of reality that are objectively good. Namely, that there are certain elements of the world that are good independently of our feelings about them, these include liberty, materiality, beauty, connection, and health.

**Liberty**

Among the components of happiness as a state of well-being that make up Objective List Theory, liberty is one candidate. For present purposes, we may define liberty or freedom as the maximisation of personal choice in that rational individuals have the opportunity and the autonomy to choose how to lead their lives at each moment minimally free from the constraint and interference of others. The value of liberty is evident in returning to the thought-experiment of the dream machine. The value of the dream machine is that it endows users with unlimited free choice. It can enable you to be whomever you wanted, in whatever circumstance you wanted, knowing it is artificial or not. Choice is the defining characteristic of the dream machine. If the machine offered merely a large variety of pre-programmed experiences, it would not be satisfactory to lead life within it. A future that is already known is very similar indeed to the past. The dream machine thought experiment serves to indicate the importance of liberty as part of happiness. However, readers will not need a thought experiment to appreciate how their own liberty connects to their happiness.

The value of near unlimited freedom is almost self-evident just as is the evil of serfdom, slavery, and subservience to a higher authority. But, beyond intuition, it is useful for our purposes to identify instances where happiness and freedom have empirically confirmed relationships. There are several of these examples. A paper in 2017 investigated the compatibility of freedom and happiness in nations by assessing the results of data gathered in the World Database of Happiness. This study found that freedom and happiness are positively correlated in contemporary nations and, more importantly, that there was no pattern of declining happiness returns, which suggests that freedom has not passed its maximum in the freest countries (Rahman, 2018).

Another study looked at the connection between freedom and happiness at a more micro-level using data on 41 nations from the World Value Survey 1995–1997. This study confirmed that people are happier in social contexts where they have more freedom (persons in higher power positions, persons with higher incomes, persons in free market and democratic societies, and persons in less stratified societies) (Haller & Hadler, 2006).

Another study quantitatively confirmed the freedom-happiness connection with reference to the experience of developing countries. This study looked at data for 46 nations in the early 1990's and found only positive correlations between freedom and happiness (Veenhoven, 2000). Importantly, this study qualified that freedom is related to happiness only when 'opportunity' and 'capability' coincide given that evidence showed having poor access to material goods in developing countries prevented the liberty-happiness connection from being fulfilled.

Even in collectivist countries that score low on economic and social freedom, the liberty-happiness correlation endures as confirmed by a study showing that Chinese adolescents are happiest when they believe that they have free will and determine their own lives (Wang et al., 2017). In this regard, it would be remiss not to recognise the relationship between time and freedom. Individuals need free time to exercise freedom. There is a perception, and for some a reality, that they live lives constantly with too many things to do and an insufficient amount of time in which to do them. A 2020 study indicated that time poverty shows a negative association with perceived well-being, physical health and productivity (Giurge et al., 2020). In total, then, the connection between happiness and liberty can be theoretically and quantitatively established. Liberty can be considered an objective component to an objective definition of well-being.

### Materiality

Material wealth is another component of happiness as a state of well-being as part of the Objective List Theory. Similar to the value of liberty, the fundamental goodness of material wealth is also largely self-evident. It would be challenging if not impossible to argue that a life of absolute poverty and scarce access to essentials like food, shelter, and health could be in any sense more desirable than a life of unlimited choice and variety in material consumption. Individuals would always prefer the latter given the choice. Rich people have the greatest access to material security and consumption. Therefore, it is reasonable to expect that richer individuals are happier compared to individuals who lack material security.

This connection between happiness and material wealth is verifiable with regard to empirical data. For example, a 2020 study looking at happiness data from 1972–2016 found that associations between income and happiness were linear, with no tapering off at higher levels of income (Twenge, 2020). In other words, there was no limit to the extent to which greater wealth could produce happiness. There is a long-established view that money cannot buy happiness. Indeed, many readers are likely to have heard this adage proclaimed from time to time in their own lives. Unfortunately, it is simply not true. Money does, in fact, buy happiness. A study in 2020 looked at 1,725,994 experience-sampling reports from 33,391 employed US adults and found that experienced and evaluative well-being increased linearly with income, with an equally steep slope for higher earners as for lower earners (Killingsworth, 2021). In other words, those earning $175,000 were less happy than those earning $250,000, and so on.

Although data does not exist to establish this view, it is intuitive that there is an upper limit to happiness and materiality. For instance, there is no significant difference in terms of what one can buy when comparing an individual that commands 10 billion dollars and an individual worth 100 billion dollars. In any case, it is clear that wealth matters. In terms of material fulfilment, one study indicates that individuals must spend their greater wealth properly if it is to produce an effect in happiness. Individuals must spend on products or services that match their personality if the greatest effect on their happiness is to occur (Matz et al., 2016). In terms of material security, individuals that have significant cash-on-hand are more likely to be happier. One study showed that access to direct money is of unique importance to life satisfaction, above and beyond the particular state of an individual's raw earnings, investments, or level of indebtedness (Ruberton et al., 2016).

In terms of personal security, the materiality surrounding levels of human development and human capital also matters to happiness. The UN Human Development Index is formed of data measuring average achievement in individuals' life expectancy, literacy, and GDP per capita (it includes three dimensions: living long and healthy lives, having knowledge, and a decent standard of living). Evidence shows that individuals living in nations that have higher values of the human development index also have higher life evaluations (Hall & Helliwell, 2014). The reason for this relationship could be that these individuals have a greater degree of material security at an internal (relating to their own capacity to secure materials to satisfy their needs and wants) and external (relating to living in a society that offers them opportunity to pursue materiality) level. In total, the connection between happiness and materiality can be theoretically and quantitatively established. Materiality can be considered an objective, yet culturally mediated, component to an objective definition of well-being.

**Beauty**

Another component of a definition of happiness as part of the Objective List Theory is beauty. Beauty is the quality of a thing that renders it intuitively pleasurable to perceive. Readers, in thinking of beauty, may conjure up in their minds images of particular star-related phenomena, scenes of natural panorama, colorful plants and wildlife, attractive individuals, and human-made art objects. While it is intuitive that beauty and happiness are interconnected, there is debate about whether beauty is an objectively discernible quality an object or experience can take on. Some individuals would argue that there is no such thing as beauty per se and that beauty is only a subjective and culturally-determined perception that varies between people. For instance, it is the perspective of the famous rationalist philosopher Immanual Kant who argued that, "taste is fundamentally subjective, that every judgment of beauty is based on a personal experience, and that such judgments vary from person to person" (Sartwell, 2017). Readers will likely recall the time-honored adage that beauty is in the eye of the beholder.

Certainly, it would be challenging to argue that beauty has no relation to culture and that our conceptions of beauty are not subjective to one degree or another. However, it should be clear by reference to example that the world is full of things that are in themselves beautiful and that contribute to the happiness and well-being of individuals that perceive them. We suggest that the evidence for this claim is that individuals have a capacity to identify beauty prior to commanding rational capacity or having personal experience that enables them to pass a considered judgment on the world which surrounds them.

Evidence in a variety of studies has shown that infants prefer to look at physically attractive human faces when they are paired with physically less attractive human faces, that this preference does not change based on ethnicity, and that this preference extends to animal faces as well (Quinn et al., 2008). Another scientist studying infant perceptions of beauty identified that they extend beyond visual perception. Another researcher investigating perceptions of beauty suggested that infants prefer to hear Vivaldi played forward as intended instead of backward, and yet these infants have no rational capacity to appreciate the structure or form of music (Radford, 2008). Furthermore, although studies do not exist to establish this claim, we suspect that infants would also prefer classically beautiful environments and objects as opposed to those things considered ugly or those things that require education and special knowledge to appreciate.

In the case of adults, happiness is higher in beautiful settings. Evidence also shows that happiness is reported higher in more scenic environments, even after controlling for a range of variables such as potential effects of the weather and the activity an individual was engaged in at the time (Seresinhe et al., 2019). Other evidence from the Netherlands indicates that happiness is highest at natural coasts and in areas with low-lying natural vegetation and that peacefulness, fascination, and scenic beauty are all predictors of happiness (DeVries, 2021). It is interesting to observe that humans have appreciated beauty even in their distant and highly difficult past, as evidenced by the fact that nomadic and hunter/gatherer tribes made spearheads that were symmetrical as seen in the Acheulean handaxe symmetry in the Middle Pleistocene period which occurred tens of thousands of years ago. Our distant and comparatively under-developed ancestors, even in harsh environments, were willing to dedicate their limited energy to producing symmetrical tools simply because they looked more beautiful (as opposed to having a higher utility for hunting prey) (White & Foulds, 2018).

The fact that beauty can be recognised without rationality, without experience, and without conscious awareness of it indicates that there are objectively beautiful qualities of objects beyond whatever sense of beauty emgerfecs from socialisation and social construction. But what is the nature of these qualities? Perhaps the best definition for those objective parts of beauty come from Aristotle who wrote that "The chief forms of beauty are order and symmetry and definiteness, which the mathematical sciences demonstrate in a special degree" (Sartwell, 2017). Order and symmetry are produced spontaneously and intentionally. These qualities can be used to create beautiful objects and experiences both naturally and artificially via the application of rationality. Take, for instance, the fact that in nature there is recurrence of harmony and proportion in patterns of design. The best known example of this principle is the recurrence of the Fibonacci sequence (mathematically speaking that each number is the sum of the two preceding ones) which manifests in how flowers grow petals and even in the arrangement of the human genome (Lamb & Shields, 2021). Other famous manifestations of symmetry in human environments include the pyramids of Egypt and Greek monuments such as the Parthenon.
The reason for why beauty produces happiness in all these examples is likely found in human evolution. Healthy and nutritious plants form symmetrical leaves and fruit. Likewise, healthy and genetically strong individuals have symmetrical faces. An appreciation for beauty is hard-wired into the human mind from birth because it functions to indicate what kinds of foods, places, and people are evolutionarily attractive. In sum, it is reasonable to conclude that there are elements to our perception of beauty as an objective phenomena that are integral to happiness.

## Connection

Another important component of an objective concept of happiness is the connection an individual has to the world around them. In a broad sense, connection may refer to one's perception or feeling of having a close relationship to one's environment and to other individuals within it. Humans, as a species, have developed and evolved over tens of thousands of years in social environments where rational cooperation determined one's success within the bounds of a community. Indeed, one anthropological investigation into the evolution of human culture and cooperation concluded that our modern success as a species may have depended on natural selection favoring genes that lead to the expression of pro-social behaviours that are likely to bring about social connection and friendship (Boyd & Richerson, 2009). If this is true, social connection is part and parcel of the biological structure of human brains themselves. One may conclude that there exists a built-in need for some connection between oneself and others.

In support of this proposition is quantitative research that concludes that friendship is a significant determinant of happiness. Evidence suggests that individuals can become happier when they have social outlooks to life, interact with more people more often, and also have conversations that are meaningful and personally relevant (Sun et al., 2019). Other studies have looked at happiness and friendship while controlling for the impact of an individual's personality. A study in 2007 found that friendship accounted for 58% of the variance in happiness and that friendship quality (in essence the level of connection between friends) was a better predictor of happiness than an individual's personality or number of friends (Demir & Weitekamp, 2007).It is clear that friendship is an important connection for happiness. Moreover, it would be reasonable to extrapolate these findings to conclude that communities of individuals that are well-connected within a neighborhood or city tend to produce greater happiness than those that are closed-off and lonely.

Apart from social connectedness, happiness can also result in one perceiving their connection to nature and the world. A study in 2014 found that people are happier when they have a connection with nature in regard to their cognitive representation of themselves (being of nature), their connectedness to nature (being connected to nature), and nature relatedness (being cognitively and physically situated within a dynamic natural context) (Capaldi et al., 2014). Connection, on the whole, appears fundamental to a happy human experience and may be integrated in our DNA.

**Health**

Finally, and perhaps most clearly, health is fundamental to happiness. This is intuitively clear. All the liberty, material security, beauty, or connection in the world would fail to offset the cost of sickness. When one is sick, the desire for well-being overrides all others. People who are sick are generally not happy. The World Health Organization defines health as possessing "a state of complete physical, mental and social well-being and not merely the absence of disease or infirmity." (Sartorius, 2006). Certainly, health thus defined is important to happiness. There is strong clinical evidence to support the claim of there being an association between physical diseases and disorders on the one hand and depression and anxiety on the other (Clarke & Currie, 2009).

Interestingly, the relationship between health and happiness goes both ways. On the one hand, healthier people are happier. This was confirmed by a 2011 study at Cornell that showed self-reported healthy people were 20 percent happier than average and that self-reported unhealthy people are 8.25 percent less happy than average (Guo & Hu, 2011). On the other hand, happier people also become healthier in several ways. For one thing, happier people are more active and eat healthier foods compared to unhappy people (Sapranaviciute, 2017). Happy individuals also appear to have enhanced immune responses to viral infection than individuals that are unhappy. A study in 2003 involving giving participants a low-grade virus and studying their immune response. This study found that the happiest individuals were 3 times less likely than the least-happy individuals to get a cold (Cohen et al., 2003). Happier people may also have lower risk of heart disease caused by persistent high blood pressure. A study in 2014 showed that the happiest people had a 48% reduced probability for heart failure compared to the least-happy (Kim et al., 2014). For all these reasons, it is unsurprising that happier people tend to live longer and healthier lives compared to those who are unhappy (Chida & Steptoe, 2008).

In conclusion, the purpose of this chapter was twofold. First, it looked briefly at different philosophical conceptions of happiness. Next, it made the case that there exists an objective list of elements of life that contribute to happiness and are worthwhile in themselves. In particular, this chapter argued for the objective elements of the list to consist of liberty (a maximum scope of free choice), materiality (access to material wealth and security), beauty (interaction with classically beautiful entities), connection (a sense of being joined in relationships with friends and community), and health (complete well-being). While this chapter argues for this objectivist position, it is important to note that this chapter does not intend to deny the view that happiness is subjective. There can be no doubt that the manner in which individuals perceive their lives has profound impacts on their happiness. It is reasonable that an individual could be sub-optimally happy, despite that all their desires grounded in this chapter's proposed objective list are fulfilled.

In order to address why this might be, we may turn to investigating happiness as a social phenomenon. In particular, the sociological discipline of social constructivism focuses on how jointly-established understandings and assumptions of reality are created and shared. It looks at how, as defined by the mere perception of a reality, whether true or not, can have real effects and consequences. Clearly, there is great power for ideas to influence human happiness. This is perhaps truer today more than ever before given that modern society is one that is deeply seated in symbolic and manufactured environments and individuals' self-concepts are heavily shaped by their interactions with others. Later in this book, the social influences and impacts of (un)happiness will be explored in greater detail. For now, to summarise, this chapter attempted to leverage a history of philosophy to objectively perceive elements of our world that constitute a happy life. In the next chapter, this book will look more deeply at particular cultural conceptions of happiness.

# Chapter 2: Western Perspectives on Happiness

*"Happiness is the meaning and the purpose of life, the whole aim and end of human existence."*
                                                      *- Aristotle*

As we have begun to see, and will continue to see over the remainder of this book, there are many different perspectives and theories on some of the most basic and presumably universal concepts, such as happiness. Despite their presence around the world and apparent simplicity, many of these fundamental concepts have been the topics of discourse and research for millenia, as people have tried to truly come to terms with what these most basic aspects of being human truly entail. So far, we have introduced this idea through the previous discussion of various theories of happiness. Taking this a step further, the next two chapters will focus on the changing and varied perceptions regarding this same fundamental to both living a good life, as well as to the human experience in general: happiness.

Alongside and amid no small number of shared aspects of the human experience and of everyday life in a modern world, many variations between cultures can and have been identified. While many common examples like the differences in individualism and collectivism between eastern and western cultures - where the former as a group tend towards collectivism, and the latter group tends towards individualism - are taught and known, at least at a particularly surface level, others are more surprising to hear about. Though ultimately an emotion shared by people everywhere, conceptualizations of happiness and related topics have been found to differ between eastern and western cultures (Joshanloo, 2014). Furthermore, ideas about what it means to be happy, and about whether it is even possible to achieve true happiness in this life, have changed over time within the separate cultural groups. Though there has been a great deal of overlap and similarities across cultures and time regarding perceptions and definitions of happiness, there have also been notable differences, especially in more modern times (Oishi et al., 2013), but also across the history of these cultures and the history of happiness itself. As such, given these historical and modern cultural differences, this chapter will begin the exploration of the various perspectives of happiness by first exploring the history and changing meaning of happiness in the West, (presently denoting the majority of Europe and the Americas, but tracing its roots back to ancient Greece and Rome) and two of the dominant influences on it, the so-called Athenian and Judeo-Christian views.

## The Athenian View and Ancient Greek Perceptions of Happiness

Although quite different from what many readers might think of when they consider what happiness means to them, historically, happiness and the words used for it had less to do with positive affect or states, and was more focused around ideas of being fortunate and lucky in both western and eastern cultures (Oishi et al., 2013). Though there are examples of this in both eastern and western cultures in antiquity, for the purposes of this chapter we will focus in on the ancient Greek term eudaimonia - a term often translated as meaning 'happiness.' Breaking down the etymology of the word, historian McMahon observed that the word was a combination of the Greek eu meaning good, and daimon meaning god or demon. From this, it was concluded that the word inherently had a sense of fortune implied when it was used, since the idea of having a 'good demon' on your side, looking out for you like a sort of guardian angel, is essentially one of luck and being fortunate enough to have the divine favour you in this way. As such, as far back as the time of the ancient Greek poet Hesiod, where the term eudaimonia was first used, happiness meant something that was done to us and which was out of our control - something outside of human agency (Oishi et al.).

Despite this dominant view as happiness essentially being something done to us which was held by the majority of poets and thinkers at the time, and the basic etymological breakdown of the word just discussed, it was not too long before some began to argue against this notion of happiness, namely the trio of famous ancient greek philosophers known to just about everyone at this point, Socrates, Plato, and Aristotle, the latter of which, as will soon be seen, had the greatest and longest lasting impact on western ideas of happiness.

Before getting to the most influential of the three (regarding this topic anyways) it is worth looking first at Socrates and Plato. Always one for disagreeing with commonly held views and beliefs, Socrates did not accept the widely held and somewhat fatalistic view of happiness as good fortune or favour from the divine. Instead, Socrates held a more agentic view of happiness, and argued that education and knowledge, and the appreciation of these, were necessary for one to come to happiness later in life. In short, Socrates essentially argued that happiness comes from a life spent philosophizing - from appreciating the beauty in the world and spending time in the later years contemplating and focusing oneself on philosophy (Oishi et al., 2013). While perhaps also not what many would think of when considering a happy life, this movement towards some amount of agency over one's own happiness - the idea that you need to do certain things or live a certain, 'good' way - is still likely more familiar to the modern western views of happiness than the originally almost entirely fortune centered eudaimonia.

Along this same line of thought are Plato's views on the matter, where he argues somewhat more generally that happiness comes from an individual's drive towards their completion, and towards their desires of beauty through their creative expressions and work (Frede, 2017). Additionally, both Socrates and Plato argued that virtues were important to achieving eudaimonia, with the latter arguing that people naturally felt unhappy when they did something they actively knew to be wrong, and using this argument to create an idea of happiness which stemmed from both moral thought and behaviour (Moore, 2021). Despite what has been shared here though, neither Plato nor Socrates ultimately gave a great deal of direction regarding happiness and its pursuit beyond these points and ideas (Frede). In order to find further direction, we have to look one generation of ancient Greek philosophers down, and see what Aristotle had to say on the matter - and why it lasted nearly a millennium after him.

Like Plato and Socrates before him, Aristotle focused heavily on morality and the virtues he identified as being related with it. Also much like his two predecessors, Aristotle argued that happiness stemmed from this sort of moral, and philosophical lifestyle (Oishi et al., 2013; Snyder, Lopez, & Pedrotti, 2010). However, though the three philosophers ended up arguing largely from the same side regarding happiness, with Aristotle largely expanding upon the work and views of Plato and Socrates before him regarding the meaning and achievement of eudaimonia, Aristotle was not in complete agreement with them. To start, though it is unlikely that Plato or Socrates entirely dismissed the notion of fortune inherent in the word eudaimonia when they made their arguments, Aristotle was much quicker than the other two to focus on the external factors - simply in conjunction with what the individual has the ability to do, unlike most of the thinkers before the three of them.

This distinction between the views of Aristotle and his predecessors is perhaps best displayed with the story of Priam, a story which was discussed by both Aristotle and Plato, albeit to different ends. The short of the story is that Priam was a man who was virtuous his whole life, yet lost everything near and dear to him due to a war. In Plato's view, Priam had lived a eudaimonic life because of how he had chosen to live it. Yet, Aristotle argued that Priam had ultimately not lived one, due to his severe lack of good fortune (Oishi et al.). Herein lies the difference between the two dominant views of happiness and eudaimonia within the Athenian view, which is the view that happiness is the end product of a virtuous and somewhat lucky life.

Though both Plato and Aristotle argued for this virtue based view, Aristotle kept a greater emphasis on the fortune one needed to live a eudaimonic life, while Socrates and Plato argued for a more agentic concept of eudaimonia within the Athenian view. However, despite the fact that Plato's stance is likely more common in the modern west, and that people would likely say that Priam did everything he could to pursue and reach happiness by the definitions of the time, it was Aristotle's view which would carry on with greater impact. Though we would eventually come to a more hedonistic view of happiness in the west, Aristotle's mixed view of happiness as something that one could work towards, yet ultimately not achieve entirely on one's own, would be the one to last, and to eventually be picked up and modified by religious philosophers.

## The Judeo-Christian View and Western Religious Perceptions of Happiness

Although a lot was still left to be changed between the time of Aristotle's eudaimonia and the contemporary western views and perceptions of happiness, the changes seemed to take place over a much longer period of time relative to the rapid changes witnessed in ancient Greece. While over the course of three generations of philosophers ideas of happiness changed from it being something entirely out of human control to something possible for those few who would dedicate themselves to Aristotle's aforementioned proposed life of virtue and philosophy, it would take over 1000 years before the next step towards modern western notions of happiness. Of course, with that being said it is worth noting that it only took half as long before we saw evidence of steps backwards, at least in terms of our present topic. It would not be until St. Thomas Aquinas in the 13th century that we began to see an evolution of Aristotle's eudaimonia take place.

When we left our discussion of ancient Greek philosophers and their early takes and philosophies on happiness, we left with Aristotle's view that happiness was a sort of end goal that could be achieved through dedication - as well as a fair deal of good fortune. Over the years though, with the rise of Judeo-Christian religions throughout, views on the pursuit of happiness in this life began to change. By the time of St. Augustine and his book The City of God sometime during the beginnings of the 5th century, there was evidence not of simply a return to the pre-Aristotle, almost entirely fortune based concept of eudaimonia, but of several steps past the ancient Greek views on the matter, as now it was argued that we had no agency in our happiness, and that a pursuit of happiness during our time here on earth was not even a possibility - fortunate or otherwise (Oishi et al., 2013). Beyond this declaration of pursuing earthly happiness as essentially a fool's errand, St. Augustine additionally went so far as to say that true happiness was completely out of reach during our time here; not only was any pursuit of happiness doomed from the start, but had anyone somehow managed to beat the odds it wasn't even in the realm of possibilities that what they would find at the end of their search was really, true happiness. With the dominance of Christianity in the early history of the west - and throughout much of the rest of its history too - it seems somewhat surprising that we moved past this sort of full stop in earthly attempts at happiness. And yet, in about as long a period after Augustine as there was between Aristotle in ancient Greece and himself in the early 5th century, we eventually find our shift back on track towards our modern views of happiness.

A mere eight centuries after St. Augustine's arguments against any and all earthly attempts at happiness, we find the views set to change yet again, this time starting the west onto the path that we will be able to follow all the way to modernity. Before this though, we have the contributions of St. Thomas Aquinas in the 13th century. Though Aquinas held some of the same beliefs as his predecessor Augustine, namely that a perfect happiness is not possible during our mortal lives, he went a very different direction with his arguments from there. Rather than taking this sentiment and using it to conclude that no pursuit of happiness while alive will amount to anything, Aquinas instead held that we could in fact achieve a sort of imperfect or partial happiness during our time here (Oishi et al., 2013; "Thomas Aquinas," n.d.). To Aquinas, this sort of pseudo - yet achievable - happiness that could be reached by all during their time on earth was essentially an imperfect reflection of the perfect, true happiness that both he and Augustine argued would be found in the afterlife. In addition to arguing that at least some amount of happiness was attainable for humanity during their lives, Aquinas also made clear the process we play in the pursuit of his new conception of eudaimonia, one he ultimately defined as a realization of truth, and as becoming closer to God (or at least as close to these as we can get while still alive) (Oishi et al., 2013; "Thomas Aquinas," n.d.).

In order for us to do what had been deemed impossible for the past 800 or so years, Thomas Aquinas, much like Aristotle far before him, held that we had to pursue a life of certain virtues (Oishi et al., 2013). As perhaps is no surprise at this point, Aquinas was in part influenced by Aristotle's philosophy and his views on eudaimonia, even arguing many of the same 11 virtues as Aristotle - for context, some examples of those put forward by Aristotle are courage, moderation, generosity, and even friendship (Snyder, Lopez, & Pedrotti, 2010). However, Aquinas didn't simply dust off Aristotle's millennium old ideas and pass them off as his own; in addition to the virtues prescribed by Aristotle, Aquinas put forward three additional virtues that were needed in order to find happiness in this life, those revealed by Christ to humanity: faith, hope, and charity(/love, depending on who you ask) (Snyder, Lopez, & Pedrotti, 2010; "Thomas Aquinas," n.d.). The exact virtues and number of them which Aquinas put forward in his version of eudaimonia varies slightly depending on where you look, but ultimately whether Aquinas took all 11 of Aristotle's and added his own or trimmed the list down before adding his heavenly virtues doesn't matter in our discussion here. In the end, Aquinas took the views of Augustine before them, and used them in conjunction with Aristotle's to shift western views of happiness back towards the agentic and within the realm of possibility. But more so than this, Aquinas actually broadened the idea of eudaimonia left behind by Aristotle. No longer was some form of happiness available to only those fortunate few who also followed the virtuous and philosophical life set out by Plato and Aristotle, but instead after Aquinas it was available to everyone who earnestly attempted to become closer with God.

By the 16th century, Martin Luther took it even one step further, arguing that it wasn't wrong to be happy, and that people (namely Christians) should be happy (Oishi et al., 2013). At that point, over the span of just above two millenia, the western view of happiness went from being something entirely luck based, to being partially in our control, to being marked an impossibility, all the way back to being achievable again, and by Luther's time even outright encouraged. Happiness had gone from being only available to the fortunate and gifted few, to being available to none during this life, to being available and encouraged for all. At this point, how we got from Luther's addition to the present day may have started to become clear, as with each step after Augustine the western view of happiness became more agentic, and more widely achievable. That being said though, there is still a bit of history left to be covered, as we see in short how the western view went through its final changes over the last few centuries between Luther and now.

## Into Modernity and Contemporary Western Perceptions of Happiness

A century or so after the influence of Luther, the west found itself in the Enlightenment era, which began to move happiness away from the religious meanings of it from Aquinas and Luther, and instead shifted it towards the secular (Oishi et al., 2013). By the time of philosopher Immanuel Kant in the 18th century, the gradual change of happiness from something that happens to us to something that we make happen, which has been shown across the millenia, was in full swing. With Kant, the west switched from Aristotle's eudaimonia to Plato's, as Kant emphasized a focus on what could be controlled, ultimately leading to the dominant and very agentic modern view of eudaimonia and its sort of virtuous and earned happiness. Then, later in the same century the pursuit of happiness was included in Thomas Jefferson's Declaration of Independence as an absolute right, further pushing the idea of happiness away from the luck-based meaning of old. Although, it is not entirely agreed upon what exactly Jefferson meant when he said "happiness" in his declaration; whether he meant a pursuit of wealth and property or a more private and civic form of happiness or something else altogether (Oishi et al.), Jefferson's inclusion of the pursuit of happiness essentially set the foundation for the American dream that most of us are familiar with now, and which enticed so many over the course of the next few centuries. Then, by the early 20th century, the ancient Greek meaning of happiness was all but gone, with America fully embracing an agentic and controllable notion of happiness set out by Jefferson and many before him, and exploring this version of happiness as the world began to grow into what it is today. With all of this said, though, it is worth noting that, despite the ancient Greek roots of happiness and the virtue centered eudaimonic view on it, some have argued that the modern western view of happiness strayed away from its roots sometime ago, and that instead of just an agentic, controllable eudaimonia, the enlightenment actually led the west to a hedonistic definition of happiness (Joshanloo, 2014).

Although happiness has been defined by and centered around the virtue and meaning-heavy Greek concept of eudaimonia (albeit with varying levels of emphasis on fortune over time) a very pleasure and self focused view of happiness can be seen throughout the west (Joshanloo, 2014). This focus on and pursuit of positive affect over negative affect defines hedonism: "the doctrine that pleasure or happiness is the sole or chief good in life" ("Hedonism," n.d.). In other words, hedonism is a view of happiness entirely focused on the acquisition of pleasure and other positive emotions, and one which stands in stark contrast to any variant of the virtuous eudaimonia. In fact, so at odds was hedonism to the ancient concept of eudaimonia that Aristotle actually addressed it, condemning the pursuit of happiness in this way as something fit only for the truly vulgar, as he equated it to pursuing the life of an animal. Despite this strong condemnation, and the lasting similar sentiments present over much of the history of the west, this view of happiness and well-being can be seen throughout modern western culture, even being present in western psychological conceptualizations and theories of well-being and motivation, all to the point where it seems that, "in the contemporary West, happiness is defined dominantly based on the absence and presence of pleasure and certain emotions" (Joshanloo, 2014, p. 483). With all of this said, though, it is important to note that there are also considerable variations on the modern views of happiness within the west, with the greatest differences of note being between American definitions of happiness and those of other parts of the west.

## Differences Between Contemporary Western Perceptions of Happiness

While the focus of this and the next few chapters is on presenting the histories of happiness in the East and West so that the many similarities and unique differences can be displayed, some time will be briefly spent here on some of the aforementioned differences within the western definitions of happiness, and some studies which explore them. To start, an observation of particular note is one made by linguist Anna Wierzbicka, where she found that the word happy in the English language is used at a far greater rate than its use in other European languages (2004). Along similar lines, Oishi et al. (2013) conducted a study examining the dictionary definitions of happiness across 30 countries, and explored how rates of happiness correlated with various factors, including whether happiness had more or less of a luck based meaning. What they found was that, of the 30 nations, 24 of them had luck or fortune as part of their definition for happiness, with the United States being one of the six which did not, along with Ecuador, India, Spain, Kenya, and Argentina (Oishi et al.).

For our purposes here, we will for now focus in on what this variance in definition shows specifically in regards to the definition of happiness in western nations: though on the whole, western perspectives of happiness have a history which pushed towards ideas of agency and control over one's happiness, the eudaimonic roots have not been lost in all, or even necessarily many western nations conceptions of happiness. At least in the languages of some western countries, it appears the ancient Greek, fortune-based conceptualization of eudaimonia lives on, and that there is divergence within the west, and even within the same language, as is the case with Australian versus American definitions of happiness. The study did not end with this result though, as the authors went on to examine how the presence of luck in the definition of happiness correlated with a number of factors; the one most significant for this discussion, is the finding that people from nations that had luck and fortune as part of their conceptualizations of happiness reported feeling and experiencing happiness less often than those people from nations which did not (Oishi et al., 2013) - a finding in line with Wierzbicka's aforementioned linguistic work.

Further studies focusing in on the meaning and use of the word happiness by presidents of the United States in their State of the Union Addresses, and on the rate of use of the phrases 'happy nation' versus 'happy person' over time were also conducted, and found that, in line with what has previously been discussed regarding the evolution of happiness in the United States, happiness was used less in presidential speeches as the word shifted from a more collectivistic to a more individualistic sentiment, as this made it less fitting for formal speeches. It also found that, as time went on, the use of the phrase 'happy nation' declined and the use of 'happy person' increased as the United States saw its final shifts towards the modern meaning of happiness (Oishi et al., 2013) On a tangential note, as the reader may have noticed, the authors have extensively referenced Oishi et al. in this chapter. We would like to particularly recommend reading this study, as it provides a deeper, comprehensive dive into some of the points discussed in this chapter.

So, though there were likely many other figures, philosophers, and events between the inception of eudaimonia and the west's modern and arguably hedonistic concept of happiness, this is in short, the history of happiness and its many changes in the west. It is not always clear when or where, or even how, these shifts in perspectives and arguments came about, as often it is simply that there is evidence of a shift in thought past a certain point without any clear indication of the origin. Odds are that this is because, for many shifts, it was more of a process than a moment which led to the new view - even if that process was usually punctuated by some noteworthy historical figure speaking out about the changes and the views. It has hopefully been shown that happiness hasn't always been what it is to us today throughout history, and that even now there are differences in what happiness means to the multitude of different groups and people contained within what we have been referring to as the West. Of course, this is also really only half the story; though we have covered from ancient Greece to the modern day, we have only done this for the west. As such, the focus of the next chapter will be to look at the history of happiness and the people and events which dot it in the East, in order to see how similarly and yet still differently something as basic and human as the idea of happiness has evolved.

# Chapter 3: Eastern Perspectives on Happiness

*"Isn't it a joy to study and regularly practice? What's more, isn't it a joy to meet comrades from afar?"*
- Confucius

Now that we have finished our exploration of the meaning of happiness and its development in the West, it is time to move onto a similar exploration in the East. While the exact meaning of the West changed over time, initially referring to european nations and later including countries east and west of Europe which had been heavily influenced by colonization, culturally speaking the meaning of the East has stayed relatively the same: the eastern world in relation to Europe, otherwise known as the continent of Asia. Though a great deal of similarities are and have been shared across cultures and over time - especially in the case of certain human fundamentals like happiness, as was noted on a few occasions in the previous chapter - there have also been some significant differences. While happiness can certainly be considered one of many shared human experiences, what exactly it means across cultures and between individuals can and has varied greatly. As such, though far from wholly different and distinct from the meanings discussed in our exploration of the West, we will now look at how the meaning of happiness has differed in the East, as well as at the major influences which led to this meaning.

As was previously mentioned, one aspect where on average the East and West have differed is on how individualistic or collectivistic the cultures are (Joshanloo, 2014). While there is a great deal of variation within each culture, in general Eastern cultures tend to be more collectivist than Western cultures, putting reduced emphasis on the self in favor of the group. Though only one small part when considering all of the major influences that will be discussed in this chapter, this emphasis on collectivism present today is still of some significance. Though as was covered the West has adopted a more self-centered, agentic, and even hedonistic notion of happiness depending on where you look, one might recall that this was not always the case.

Originally, though Plato and Socrates argued for a greater focus on what one can do and control, the dominant western view was from Aristotle, which put a much greater emphasis on external factors in conjunction with personal agency when it came to one's own happiness. Why this is interesting to note is because, though we will see a number of similarities between the ideas of happiness across the world, this western evidence of a focus on those around you shows that, at least at the start, there did not seem to be that great of a difference between how western - specifically the ancient Greek philosophers - and eastern cultures viewed happiness. In fact, if we look as far back as within 200 years of Aristotle's life, we find evidence in the Classic of Rites that the word "fu" was used incredibly similarly to how Hesiod used the Greek eudaimonia.

With this said, what remains to be seen is how the meaning of happiness diverged from there. What events and influences led to the modern day conceptualization of happiness in the East, and how did the concept change from the happiness known millennia ago? Unlike our exploration of happiness in the West though, this chapter will not focus as greatly on the broader timeline of changes. Although the meaning of happiness did change over time in the East, many of the more significant influences happened early and around the same time, with some even happening concurrently, simply in different regions. For this reason, the changes won't be presented as a timeline or a linear development, but instead as the different parts that ultimately led into the present meaning. To begin this exploration, we will explore how Confucius and Confucianism shaped the meaning of happiness.

**Confucianism and its Influence on Happiness**

Confucianism finds its beginnings in China between the 6th and 5th centuries BCE, during the lifetime of the philosopher Confucius for whom it is named (Weiming, 2019). Although it has lasted for nearly 3000 years, with many of Confuscius's works and thoughts continuing to circulate and be shared - one of the most famous being Confucianim's golden rule of "Do not do unto others what you would not want others to do unto you" (National Geographic Society, 2020a) - it is not wholly agreed upon what Confucianism is. Though often viewed as a philosophy, religion, or both, Confucianism's exact nature is debated, as it seems to go beyond being just a philosophy, and yet does not in any way prohibit other religious affiliations. As such, it may be best to think of it more along the lines of a moral and ethical code, or as a way of thinking which provides guidelines on what is important, and on how one should live (Weiming). However, despite these potentially semantic uncertainties regarding what Confucianism should be regarded as, there is no great deal of uncertainty in its origins or the teachings of Confucius and those that came after him. For Confucius, what mattered above all else was a person's humanity, and the pursuit of moral character through education and ritual, with the aim of realizing the good in ourselves and engaging in various virtuous behaviours (National Geographic Society). Now, with this context in place, we can begin to explore how this ancient and virtue-centered worldview conceptualized and influenced what it meant to be happy.

Standing in stark contrast to the previously explored hedonistic view of happiness, which some have argued as defining the contemporary Western view of happiness, Confucius argued that happiness had little if anything at all to do with the pursuit of material pleasures. In Confucianism, no distinction is made between a happy life and a good life, but how one goes about becoming happy is particularly distinct from some modern thinking; rather than seek out pleasure and positive states in order to be happy, one should instead commit themselves to self-cultivation and the attainment of virtue, so that one may live in harmony with those around them (Joshanloo, 2014). Mencius, a later Confucian philosopher of particular note, even went so far as to describe the experience of unbelievable joy stemming from the practice of such a virtuous life (Chan, 1963).

So, with this kind of virtue based conception of joy and happiness, what kind of virtues were being taught and emphasized? While it has already been mentioned that Confucius put a great emphasis on self cultivation and working towards one's humanity, five more specific virtues have been identified which Confucius argued were essential to reaching his version of enlightenment: humanity, the duty to treat others well, etiquette and sensitivity for others, wisdom, and truthfulness (Snyder, Lopez, & Pedrotti, 2010).

Along with immediately being able to see Confucianism's golden rule partially present in the second listed virtue, it is also worth noting that this view of happiness has at least as much to do with focusing on others as it does on oneself, as everything was aimed towards the achievement of humanity and harmony.

In addition to and expanding upon these five virtues, Confucius goes further in his philosophy, and argues not only that we are capable of changing ourselves and should in the name of virtue, but that there is a difference between being virtuous for social praise and being virtuous for the sake growth; rather than simply blindly doing what is right, Confucius argued that we should rejoice in our virtue and do what is right because our pursuit of growth. And like Mencius after him, Confucius said there was joy to be gained from this, from our personal study of virtue and engagement in our social relationships ("Confucius and Happiness," n.d.). In Confucianism, happiness is not viewed as any sort of individualistic or hedonistic pursuit of pleasure or wealth, but instead is defined by these ethical desires for growth, the ethical pleasures of self-development and cultivating one's connections, and this acknowledgement and furthering of our own inherent goodness as humans (Luo, 2019).

Though this view would hardly stay static or as the whole story regarding Eastern conceptualizations of happiness, the collectivistic sentiments and focus on oneself and others equally, if not with a greater focus on the latter, carried on, and these and other teachings from Confucius remain important to many to this day. As we will see though, Confucius and Confucianism are not the only influences on the meaning of happiness in the East.

## Taoism and its Influence on Happiness

Near and around a similar time as Confucius and the rise of Confucianism is the ancient Chinese religion and philosophy of Taoism or Daoism, depending on how it was transcribed into English. Unlike the topic of the previous section, Taoism is very much regarded as both a religion and a philosophy, and is connected to the philosopher known as Lao Tzu (National Geographic Society, 2020b) - or Lao Tzi, or a number of other known but less common names, spellings, and transliterations. Lao Tzu is credited with the founding of Taoism and best known for his book the Tao-Te-Ching - translated as "The Way of Virtue" - which outlines the Taoist way of thought (Mark, 2020).

Despite his great significance to Taoism and history, little is known for certain about Lao Tzu - even his name is not known, as Lao Tzu and its many transliterations are simply an honorific meaning "Old Man" (Mark, 2020) or "Old Master" (Kaltenmark & Ames, 2020). In fact, in addition to this uncertainty, it is no longer even agreed upon amongst historians about whether Lao Tzu was a single person, or if the name was simply given to a combination of various philosophers (Mark). Worse still, in the 19th century the belief that the Tao-Te-Ching was even written by Lao Tzu came into question and if he ever existed as any number of people at all. And with no information or references that might give clue to where or when or by whom the book was written, we are largely left with just the belief it was written at some point between the 8th and 3rd century (The Editors of the Encyclopaedia Britannica, 2019). As intriguing as this lack of knowledge is though, it ultimately has little bearing on how impactful Taoism was and is, and on just what was communicated in the Tao-Te-Ching and by the Taoist philosophers who came after.

While its origins and founder are uncertain, what Taoism teaches about happiness is far from it. Similarly to Confucianism, Taoism rejects any sort of pursuit of material wealth or pleasure, often arguing for contentment above all else (Joshanloo, 2014). However, it is here in this idea of contentment that the two differ; though both Taoism and Confucianism teach that happiness comes from lives of virtue rather than personal gain and pleasure, Taoism argues that, instead of focusing on self growth and the development of oneself towards humanity through virtuous acts, we must learn to accept the world for what it is and allow it to take its course.

Expanding this idea further, it is important to note the emphasis Taoism puts on the mutually dependent dual nature of things - "all things exist in polarity" (Joshanloo, 2014, p.480), and the two opposite poles are necessary to each other, providing support and ultimately complementing their opposite. This concept of two opposite poles, of yin and yang, extends to everything, including happiness and unhappiness, and Taoism argues that in order to achieve happiness one must understand how these two poles complement each other. When one is able to see both the good and the bad as equally essential, then one can achieve happiness. So, how does Taoism say that we should go about this pursuit? To begin with, Taoism teaches that you shouldn't. While the focus is for us to align ourselves with the Tao, or the natural way and order of things, to find happiness and harmony (Mark, 2020), part of this alignment is to follow the principle of non-action - to act "effortlessly and spontaneously" (Joshanloo,

2014, p.480), and allow life to take its course. As such, no actual pursuit is necessary or encouraged.

This being said though, Taoism does still lay out a somewhat more specific goal; though the Tao is said to be something that must be experienced through the previously explained releasing of yourself to the flow of the world and not taught, four virtues are also identified for which the aim is to practice and exhibit them without effort. These four virtues are: humanity, justice, temperance, and propriety, and when one is able to practice these virtues and live virtuously, naturally, and without effort, this is when you will have reached a taoist sense of transcendence (Snyder, Lopez, & Pedrotti, 2010). More pertinent to our topic of happiness though, is that along the way, by experiencing Tao and embracing these virtues and the complementary nature of the world, this is where Taoism teaches you will find happiness.

Now we have discussed two of the main four influences on Eastern conceptualizations of happiness: the Confucian result of active virtue and self-development, and the Taoist outcome of accepting the good with the bad and the world for what it is - both arguing for a life of virtue and for a rejection of material and superficial gain in order to achieve happiness, yet differing in what the final state of happiness looks life. For the former, it is the joy of your own virtue and development, while for the latter it is the contentment of acceptance and releasing yourself to the world. While both have had great impact, and it is likely that books could be written on just the topic of happiness within these two schools of thought, our limits here require us to move on, and explore the next of the four major influences which make up the focus of this chapter.

## Buddhism and its Influence on Happiness

Buddhism, like the two major influences on Eastern views of happiness already addressed, traces its origins back to some time between the 6th and 4th century BCE in what is now part of modern-day Nepal with the birth of the Buddha (Lopez, 2020). The Buddha was born Siddhartha Gautama of Shakya, and there are many myths and stories surrounding his birth. However, despite these stories the basic, more general facts of the Buddha's life are known and agreed upon: Siddhartha Gautama was born into a wealthy family, and yet despite his life of wealth and luxury, and his father's attempts to shield him from the ugliness of the world, Siddhartha went out and experienced a variety of the less pleasant aspects of life ("Buddha And The Path To Happiness - An Overview," n.d.). Through these experiences, and his encounter with a man who by choice abstained from every worldly pleasure and yet found contentment, Siddartha renounced his own comfortable life in search of greater meaning, leading him to go and develop his philosophy and become the Buddha.

Simply and somewhat quickly put, the Buddha realized a couple of important facts about life and living following his renouncing and subsequent meditations. First, the Buddha found that one should choose to go through life following the 'Middle Path', or moderation, rather than in pursuit of either of the extremes of great indulgence or complete self-denial. Second, that life is inherently Dukkha or suffering, and is full of dysfunction and illusions, and thankfully third, that there is a solution. While there is quite obviously much more that the Buddha learnt and taught, these are the key aspects that will help to explore and explain how Buddhism presents happiness and its achievement.

Once more, Buddhism stands counter to hedonistic notions of happiness through pleasure and indulgence, arguing for moderation as the beginning of one's route to enlightenment. With this being said though, nothing worldly actually ends up factoring into the Buddhist meaning of happiness, nor in its achievement. From the Buddhist view of happiness, "happiness is achieved when a person can perceive the true nature of reality, unmodified by the mental constructs we superimpose upon it" (Ricard, 2014, p.14). Though previously put as suffering, the original meaning of Dukkha is actually more along the lines of 'mental dysfunction,' and refers to the Buddhist idea that much of what we suffer in life comes from our own attachments and false conceptions regarding ourselves and the world. As such, being able to remove ourselves from these mental constructs and leave them behind is how one achieves happiness. There is of course more to it than that, as the Buddha described something called the 'Eightfold Path', which is a systematic way to essentially escape our own ignorance, which helps one to escape our Dukkha and achieve not only happiness, but enlightenment ("Buddha And The Path To Happiness - An Overview," n.d.).

One powerful illusion put forward by Buddhism, one credited with being a primary source of our unhappiness, is the notion of our own separate, and defined self (Joshanloo, 2014). Buddhism argues that others are extensions of ourselves, and denounces acts of focusing upon oneself, favouring instead self-renunciation and detachment from craving. As is likely obvious by this point, the Buddhist notion of happiness requires a fair deal of work, as one is required to challenge and denounce many of our ideas regarding the world and even ourselves in order to reach enlightenment. As mentioned though, the Buddha offered his Eightfold Path to get there - a system that can be used to identify eight different paths that need to be taken and addressed in order to eliminate one's ignorance ("Buddha And The Path To Happiness - An Overview," n.d.). The end goal of this system is ultimately to reach enlightenment and Nirvana, where the true nature of everything is known and one is freed from any worldly desires.

In order to aid Buddhists towards this goal, four additional virtues known as the 'Brahma Viharas,' as well as methods to reach them, were taught by the Buddha. The four virtues are maitri (love), karuna (compassion), mudita (joy), and upeska (equanimity/peace of mind) (Snyder, Lopez, & Pedrotti, 2010). Though there are meditation practices which help develop these virtues or states of mind, ultimately they are achieved through removing oneself from desire, providing additional things to work towards to help one reach Nirvana. The Eightfold Path helps to reach these states so that, once you have, you will be able to detach from every worldly desire and need; for Buddhism, the quelling of one's mental dysfunction, and this subsequent attainment of such mental peace, is what happiness is ("Buddha And The Path To Happiness - An Overview").

With this understanding of Buddhism, there is only one major influence on the Eastern views of happiness left to explore. So far within each section, despite the many substantial differences in the paths towards and final definitions of happiness present between the three influences looked at, there has been a consistent theme of a rejection of the self for any reason other than growth. Along these same lines, each influence has also stood opposite hedonistic ideas of happiness, with all of them favouring the alignment of oneself with one set of virtues or another in order to live life as one should; rather than focusing on personal pleasure and enjoyment, each influence has argued for a happiness not defined by the momentary, but instead for a happiness defined by who and how you are in relation to the world around you. Though the last influence will present a definition and view of happiness unique from those already discussed, we shall find a similar thread running through it.

## Hinduism and its Influence on Happiness

Unlike the previous three influences, which all developed fairly concurrently with one another from relatively specific origins, the final influence has a much longer and less well established history. In addition to this substantial difference, Hinduism itself is also less so a single religion or philosophy, and is instead composed of a variety of philosophies, beliefs, and traditions (van Buitenen et al., 2020; Joshanloo, 2014). To top it all off, Hinduism is also quite possibly the oldest known religion, with some of the oldest of its cumulative texts potentially dating as far back as between the 2nd and 3rd millennium BCE, placing some of its roots around 4000 years ago (van Buitenen et al., 2020; History.com Editors, 2021). Needless to say, this makes Hinduism - or at least its earliest parts - a couple thousand years older than any of the other Eastern or Western influences discussed over the past two chapters. As such, only a small portion of this considerable history can be addressed in this chapter.

To begin, despite the uncertain origins and lack of a single person who can be pointed to as founder, scholars believe Hinduism originated somewhere in the Indus Valley - near present day Pakistan - between 2300 and 1500 BCE (History. com Editors, 2021). At that point, cultures merged and influenced each other, and scholars believe what came to be known as Hinduism started as a result of this. Then, some 1000 years later, Buddhism rose out of it (as the Buddha himself was born into a Hindu family) (History.com Editors). Finally, another 1500 or so years later, the name Hinduism was coined by British writers in the 19th century for the collection of related and varied philosophies and traditions (van Buitenen et al., 2020). This of course is a criminally concise overview of the history of Hinduism, but meant to simply give some sense of scale for just how old it is. However, like most things that have been around for 4000 years, there is a great deal more to this history (unfortunately, there is a great deal more which can't be covered here).

On a slightly tangential but important note, connecting the history of Hinduism, the view of happiness resulting from it which will be explored shortly, and the idea of a fortune based definition of happiness, is the meaning of one of the symbols primarily associated with Hinduism. The Hindu swastika - as in the original swastika, and not the diagonal variant adopted and ruined by the Nazi Party - symbolizes good luck, with the word itself being taken to mean either that, or 'being happy' (History.com Editors). Perhaps Hinduism, given how old it is, had something to do with the fortune based meaning of happiness that was at one point seen across the world. Regardless of whether it did or not, Hinduism's influence on conceptualizations of happiness is not limited to this.

As can probably be guessed by this point in the chapter, Hinduism's influence on Eastern conceptualizations of happiness shares some similarities with the previous influences - particularly with Buddhism, which, as just discussed, emerged out of Hinduism. This being said keep in mind the scope of Hinduism as we discuss its influences on the meaning of happiness, as not only are its influences likely not limited to what is discussed here, but due to the long and complex history, it is entirely within reason that alternative views could be found within Hinduism regarding what is about to be explored (Joshanloo, 2014).

Now we can explore what unique and similar ways Hinduism shaped conceptualizations of happiness. To begin, one significant difference between Hinduism and the previous three influences is that there are essentially two notions of happiness presented in Hinduism: happiness that comes from pleasure and from the idea of the 'good life,' and happiness which comes from the spiritual (Nishpapananda, 2010). Though both have significance, it is this latter notion of a spiritual happiness which will be focused on here, as not only is it seen as coming after the more material happiness, it is also the more meaningful kind of happiness. For some brief context, Hinduism argues that we are composed of material and non material aspects, and that the reality at the center of everything is a universal spirit called Brahman (Joshanloo, 2014)). Additionally, Hinduism argues that at the most basic level, our non-material aspects are one and the same with Brahman, but the other material aspect of ourselves and of the world hides this truth. As such, the ultimate goal of Hinduism is for us to realize this reality and in essence become one with Brahman - a notion not entirely dissimilar to the Buddhist pursuit of enlightenment.

In order to work towards this understanding which constitutes salvation, and which allows one to escape the cycle of reincarnation when achieved, you have to free yourself from all worldly bonds allowing you to find your true self, the non-material aspect that is part of Brahman (Joshanloo, 2014). It is here that we find the meaning of happiness put forward by Hinduism, as one's joy and happiness depends entirely on how successful one is with this pursuit of the true self. As such, the happiness found in Hinduism, though involving different views and a different process, is one stemming from contentment and the living of a virtuous and full life (Joshanloo, 2014; Snyder, Lopez, & Pedrotti, 2010). More similarly to Taoism than to Buddhism though, is the emphasis Hinduism places on this understanding of the nature of everything, and this pursuit of essentially oneness with it - in this case in the knowledge and true experience of oneself as part of Brahman, as opposed to giving oneself to and becoming part of Tao. In this way, happiness comes from pushing oneself towards a virtuous life full of betterment, and from the work one undertakes in order to realize their true self, rather than from any hedonistic pleasures.

As can be seen, Hinduism shares many of the same threads that the other three major influences have: the pursuit of a virtuous life full of betterment and self-cultivation, the search for and experience of the true flow of the world, and efforts to free oneself from worldly constraints in order to understand the truth. Perhaps it is unsurprising that the oldest of the influences discussed here, and which at least one of the other influences has a direct tie to, shows these similarities. Yet, despite these common themes, each influence stands unique in how they define and present happiness, with Hinduism being no different; though sharing the similarities already discussed, Hinduism presents possibly the most spiritual view of happiness, and presents happiness as coming from developing yourself due to a desire to transcend the material world, and from releasing yourself from it in order to truly know yourself.

**Shared Themes and the Traces in Modernity**

As we have already briefly touched upon the similarities between the four major influences explored in this chapter throughout their sections, only a brief moment longer will be spent here on the topic. While many more specific similarities and commonalities can be found between the influences, there are a few broader themes of particular interest to our discussion. First, all four of the influences discussed put forth some form of virtue based notion of happiness which rejected more hedonistic ideas of pleasure and happiness. In fact, the closest any of the influences got to hedonism would arguably have been the Buddhist Middle Path, which still explicitly argues against indulgence and excess, which are staples of hedonism and the pursuit of material happiness.

In addition to the virtuousness of the various conceptions, all four influences were also spiritual to some extent or another. Even Confucianism, the arguably least spiritual of the Eastern influences, still has a focus on the cultivation of the self with an understanding and emphasis on our interconnectedness. Then lastly, though likely of the least significance, all of the conceptualizations of happiness put forward by these four influences resonate with more collectivistic ideas than individualistic, as all put at least some focus on either those around us or the general connection shared between us all. With such a long and multifaceted history of happiness coming from spirituality, faith, and the betterment of oneself often for others, it perhaps seems less surprising that happiness never took the very agentic and individual focused turn in the East that it did in the West, despite the similar starting points. Of course with that said, it is still a curiosity that something like the Aristotelian eudaimonia or the later religious pursuit of earthly happiness courtesy of Aquinas and Luther never really developed. Instead of the broad and linear progression of happiness seen over the history of the West, we find gradual and concurrent evolutions and expansions of the same shared themes of virtue and self sacrifice throughout the East.

With all of this said, we will now briefly compare what was just discussed with some of the studies examined in the previous chapter. Though the background presented in these studies focused largely on the West and the changing meaning of happiness over its history, the studies themselves explored the modern meaning of happiness in nations around the world. As noted, the majority of Western nations showed a more agentic definition of happiness, even amongst those which still included fortune as a meaning of the word (Oishi et al., 2013). The opposite was also true; though fortune was prevalent across the world in the definitions of happiness, they were also particularly common in Eastern definitions of happiness, alongside many inclusions of contentment, peace, and wellbeing. While the study itself did not focus on these themes, as the purpose was to explore the historical fortune based meaning of happiness, given our previous discussions of the influences of Confucianism, Taoism, Buddhism, and Hinduism, it is worth noting them, as themes of contentment and becoming at peace and bettering oneself and being well from it can be found at least in part across all four of them. So, though we perhaps do not see people with lives fully committed to Confucian self-cultivation or Buddhist pursuits of Nirvana, we do still see the lingering of these influences, now simply more broadly and more intermixed than they perhaps were historically.

Before closing out this exploration of the historical influences in the Eastern definitions of happiness, there are two final notes worth making. The first is a consideration of why the fortune based meaning of happiness stuck around as strong as it did in the East. Given the agentic shifts that occurred over the West's history, it is no surprise that it is more present in the East, but why is it as present as it is? Though much of the information presented here is surface level at best regarding the four influences, fortune and more specifically luck were not of great significance to any of the influences. While it is possible that these ideas simply play a larger part the deeper you look into the influences, perhaps it remained as strongly as it did because of how external many of the definitions and pursuits of happiness were; though hard work and explicit action were prescribed in some way or another by at least three of the influences - with Taoism instead arguing an involved but passive experience and understanding - all pointed outwards with this effort, with all involving the freeing or sacrifice of pleasures and worldly concerns in favour of virtue and knowledge. As such, maybe fortune stayed around in the meanings not because it was philosophically integral to them anymore, but simply because the notion that happiness came from things other than worldly pleasures and temporary states was carried on and explored for so long, so the external idea of happiness was never left behind to any great extent as it was in the West. Of course, this is just speculation.

The final note, which will be echoed throughout and significant to the next chapter's discussions, and which has already been communicated a few times now, is that these differences are not so black and white as some of this discussion may frame it. Though the explorations took the form of looking at the East and West separately, all the differences noted between these two large collections of cultures can be found within and between the people of any of the cultures (Joshanloo, 2014). As such, keep in mind that, while there are interesting and in some cases considerable differences between East and West, happiness, like many other things in life, is a human experience shared by all of us.

# Chapter 4: The Similarities and Differences between Perspectives

*"It is ... noteworthy that certain qualities are universally accepted as main ingredients of happiness."*
*- Mohsen Joshanloo*

Now that the major influences on the meaning of happiness in the East and West have been explored, along with how these meanings changed over time due to them, it is time to take a more explicit look at how the varied meanings of happiness between and within the East and West compare. In addition to this pursuit, this chapter will also introduce some of the global metrics used to measure the happiness of nations around the world, and examine how these metrics work, how the East and the West compare according to them, and how the results of these metrics relate to and differ from what has already been explored in the previous two chapters. Before we launch into any of these new topics of discourse or further examine the topics of the previous chapters though, it would be prudent to first address and answer a couple questions of some note regarding our various topics: why do we, or should we, care about these topics, and what do we get from their exploration?

While there are always arguments to be made regarding the pursuit of knowledge for knowledge's sake, these arguments have never been enough for everybody, even when it comes to justifying a pursuit as small, and in some ways trivial, as these. As such, a moment will be taken here to further argue the value of these and likely other seemingly inconsequential reflections and explorations of our shared and separate pasts and presents.

To begin, though it is likely that many of the people in our lives share similar, if not exactly identical, notions of happiness and what this word truly means, these explorations and discussions which have taken place over these past few chapters, and which will continue on throughout the rest of this chapter, help highlight the idea that things are not as static as they may seem. Though our own personal understandings of happiness as well as various similarly basic human notions may be well established to us, it can be worthwhile to remember how differently people can approach and come to understand a variety of topics. More specifically, it can pay to keep in mind that not everyone thinks the same way as us, that not all of our ideas will be shared even amongst those closest to us, and that, oftentimes, these differences can present an opportunity for some small amount of learning and growth.

What's more, explorations of our pasts, both shared and unique to ourselves, can provide us the chance to see the threads of our views and our beliefs, and how overall we got to where we are now. This discussion and acknowledgement of our unique yet related histories, even regarding something so small as 'what does happiness mean to different people,' can help provide an understanding of how different people everywhere can be from our individual selves, and why. So, though these new understandings and takeaways are not necessarily going to cause any great change, hopefully they help provide new opportunities for understanding some more about both ourselves and others. Now that that is all said and done, we can continue the exploration of how we relate and differ regarding the topic of happiness.

## Comparisons of the East and West

As has been discussed at some length by this point, the East and West have differed from one another on a variety of topics over the course of both their respective histories. However, while the focus of the past few chapters has been on the differences between the two, such as the heavier emphasis on collectivistic values in the East than in the West, and the opposite for more individualistic ones (Joshanloo, 2014), there have also been numerous similarities despite their divergent histories. Though the West developed a meaning of happiness with a greater sense of agency, a majority of nations across the East and West still incorporate at least a notion of good luck and fortune into their definitions of happiness, with many Western and Eastern nations continuing to convey this sense quite strongly (Oishi et al., 2013).

In this comparison of the two regarding the topic of happiness and its varied meanings, it is important to once more keep in mind that these differences and similarities regard nations and groups of nations as a whole, and in no way tell the story of the diversity within each of them. There are broad, sweeping differences which can be pointed to, like the argued dominance of the hedonistic view throughout the contemporary West (Joshanloo, 2014) against the continued external and balance focused views of happiness and well-being in the East (Snyder, Lopez, & Pedrotti, 2010), as well as equally broad statements of similarity which miss the nuances present within and between individual people just as much. And yet, there are indications that, regardless of these nuances, on a whole there are differences as well as similarities to be found between Eastern and Western cultures. With all this in mind, we can begin to explore some of these broadly identified differences and similarities between the cultural views and meanings of happiness.

**Differences**

In addition to the previous discussion of luck versus agency in the conceptualizations and definitions of happiness between the East and West, a number of particularly salient differences between the views can be identified. Though far from exhaustive, the exploration of these six areas of difference identified by Joshanloo (2014) through his review of the literature will compose the majority of our discussion here regarding the differences in views. To give more detail, these six "domains of difference" (Joshanloo, 2014, p. 482) identified are composed of two poles, and are presented with the observation that, broadly speaking, these poles are ideas and aspects that the East and West differ on regarding how they view happiness. The six domains identified by Joshanloo are self-transcendence versus self-enhancement, eudaimonism versus hedonism, harmony versus mastery, contentment versus satisfaction, valuing versus avoiding suffering, and relevance versus relative irrelevance of spirituality and religion. Though the exploration of each of these six domains will be brief - especially relative to the amount of detail Joshanloo discusses them in - due to the limits of the present chapter, it is important to note that there is more to each of these topics than is able to be discussed here in full.

In the split of these domains, the first pole is what aspect of the domain was identified as more relevant to Eastern views of happiness, while the second is what was found as more significant to the West. The first of the six domains, Self-Transcendence versus Self-Enhancement, largely speaks to an idea already touched upon throughout our previous discussions: the idea of collectivistic versus individualistic values. In this context, this essentially equates to the amount of focus the respective cultures puts on the individual self; in the west it is common to associate enhancing oneself and one's independence with working towards happiness and a good life, while as was seen in the various Eastern influences, the individual self is often de-emphasized if not outright dismissed on the path to happiness (Joshanloo, 2014; Snyder, Lopez, & Pedrotti, 2010). Naturally, this can influence what people prioritize in their pursuit of happiness, as well as what the end goal and the process look like to them.

The second domain is likewise familiar to us at this point, as it regards the focus put on either eudaimonism or hedonism. As was previously discussed, the Greek eudaimonia shared similarities with many of the early Eastern influences, particularly when discussing older, pre-Aristotelian notions of it. Though using this ancient Greek idea as a namesake, the eudaimonism mentioned by Joshanloo refers less to the varying views of Plato and Aristotle and more to a broader virtue based conception of happiness and well-being. And, as we found in our discussion of Eastern and Western influences and how they have affected the present views, the East retained many more of the external, virtue based ideas of happiness than the West did after its very agentic and more recently pleasure based shift in focus (Joshanloo, 2014; Oishi et al., 2013; Snyder, Lopez, & Pedrotti, 2010). Similar to the amount of emphasis put on the self, how concerned someone is with the momentary pleasures when conceptualizing happiness has a huge impact on what one would seek out in order to reach their idea of happiness.

Third is the difference between the emphasis placed on Mastery versus Harmony, specifically in reference to the world around us. As one may recall from Luther's contributions to the Judeo-Christian influence in the West, as the West went into the Enlightenment it went in with the idea that not only could people be happy in this lifetime, but that they should and deserved to (Oishi et al., 2013). Along these same lines, during the enlightenment the notion that the world was something meant for humankind to control and master came about, and led to the further emphasis on one's agency and role in their own lives and happiness (Joshanloo, 2014). Of course, it is easily remembered that nothing of the sort took place dominantly in the East; rather than control the world around them, each of the major Eastern influences discussed becoming closer to or part of the nature of the world, and existing in a state of harmony and peace with it in order to find happiness (Joshanloo; Snyder, Lopez, & Pedrotti). Naturally, working to control one's surroundings would lead to a vastly different approach to happiness than working to be one with them, and everything that underlies them.

Here the domains begin to be somewhat less familiar, though not entirely distinct from topics that came about during our previous discussions. Though the topic of contentment featured prominently throughout the Eastern influences both by name and in other words (Snyder, Lopez, & Pedrotti, 2010), the topic of satisfaction was not nearly so blatantly touched upon in our discussions of the West. Thankfully, aspects of satisfaction were discussed when exploring the presence of hedonism in the contemporary West, and the two terms contentment and satisfaction are actually quite intimately connected; though representing another domain that the two broad cultures differ on, satisfaction is part of contentment. Both the East and West place emphasis on joy, but the Eastern contentment involves much more than simply this, as it places focus on balance and acceptance of the good and the bad, as well as a far more active role in accepting the events and world around ourselves (Joshanloo, 2014). As such, though contentment is related to satisfaction, the pursuit of one over the other leads to very different ends.

The next domain, valuing versus avoiding suffering, relates intimately to the domains of eudaimonism versus hedonism and contentment versus satisfaction. Humorously, they are only related each by one pole, as the Eastern sense of contentment as involving the acceptance and active acknowledgment of the good and the bad together is related to the valuing of suffering, and the avoidance of suffering is a key feature of hedonism (Joshanloo, 2014). As such, though together they make a different domain upon which the East and West differ, it is largely composed of topics already discussed here.

This of course leaves us with only one domain, the relevance versus relative irrelevance of spirituality and religion. Though religion and spirituality were dominant factors for most of the history of both the East and West, and is still of great significance to many in the West, the influence it had on Western views of happiness waned early in the 20th century, during the previously discussed ramping up of post-enlightenment agentic views (Oishi et al, 2013). As such, the lasting impact of views and religions such as Confucianism, Taoism, Buddhism, and Hinduism in the East make it clear why the East and West are placed where they are in this domain, as spiritual and religious teachings are in no way as strongly represented in contemporary Western notions of happiness as they are in Eastern (Joshanloo, 2014; Snyder, Lopez, & Pedrotti, 2010).

Though the differences between Eastern and Western notions of happiness aren't limited to these six domains identified by Joshanloo (2014), visible as they are throughout our previous discussions (Oishi et al., 2013; Snyder, Lopez, & Pedrotti, 2010), these six domains cover a great many of them. More can be said on all of them, and further exploration can be done beyond what was already found, but broadly speaking these domains encompass at least aspects of the majority of particularly salient differences that can be found broadly between the East and the West. Of course, as was mentioned at the start of this chapter, despite the many differences between the two and the unique histories that brought them to where they are, there is more in common both on and beneath the surface than one may expect to find.

**Similarities**

Though the larger focus of the discussion regarding the meaning of happiness and its various influences in the East and West is on the differences between the two, it is still worthwhile to take a short look at in what ways the two are similar after their unique histories. While views on happiness can be quite varied between cultures - with even greater differences having been found than those discussed here, including studies finding cultural aversions to happiness (Joshanloo et al., 2013; Joshanloo & Weijers, 2014) - it's important to keep in mind some of the commonalities shared between many if not every influence and view on happiness. By looking at the similarities between the views as well as the differences, it can help us make better sense of the views themselves and their underlying reasoning, as in some cases they start from very similar points. As such, though not the primary focus of the chapter, a brief discussion of the similarities can aid in understanding the differences between the views.

As was discussed in some detail when introducing the ancient Greek concept of eudaimonia, and then again later when introducing the Eastern influences on happiness, for at least a considerable amount of time the meaning of happiness in both the East and West revolved around external factors of luck and fortune (Oishi et al., 2013). While this was largely lost over time in America and some other countries, primarily ones in the West, it was noted that it was still seen in the majority of definitions looked at. In fact, though the West was still noted for a more agentic and pleasure based concept of happiness (Joshanloo, 2014; Oishi et al., 2013), it was found that the degree of this varied quite widely within the West, as many European nations viewed happiness as a much rarer event than people in the United States had (Wierzbicka, 2004). Now, while these findings do not equate the still more agentic definition of happiness held in the majority of the West to the still very external and spiritual meaning of happiness seen throughout the East, the reminder that this external sense to the word remains in many Western nations does help to show that, at least on average, the two views are not quite as dissimilar as early discussions may have made it seem.

Along similar lines is the role of virtues in the meanings of happiness and the influences on them in both the East and West. Though there are arguments that hedonism is particularly dominant in contemporary Western notions of happiness, it seems unlikely that the emphasis on virtues was completely discarded after over 2000 years of philosophers and theologians emphasizing their importance in living happily and well (Oishi et al., 2013; Snyder, Lopez, & Pedrotti, 2010). As such, though dominant, hedonism likely is far from having a monopoly on the notions and views of happiness in the Western world, which gives yet another avenue for similarity between contemporary Eastern and Western thought on the topic.

Lastly, to close out the discussion of what is shared between the Eastern and Western views, it is worth saying again that, technically speaking, just about everything, except the furthest extremes, are when we look at the individual level - if not the extremes too. Though there is evidence of these broader cultural differences, there is also evidence of variation within the East and West due to a variety of factors and differences between individuals (Joshanloo, 2014). So, though broadly speaking the East tends one way and the West another, this is no reason to conclude that there are no Americans or Europeans who favour harmony and collectivism over pursuits of individualistic gain and mastery of their environment, nor to think that you can't find these levels of variation within nations and between the individuals in them.

## Comparisons with a Global Metric of Happiness

For the final topic of the chapter, we will briefly discuss a global metric of happiness, how it compares to what has been discussed throughout these past few chapters, and what these previous discussions suggest regarding this and potentially other global metrics. As has hopefully been made clear by this point, there are quite a few different ways to view something as basic yet ultimately subjective as happiness, with many factors and considerations that can be taken into account. Because of this, though the metric discussed will be looked at in relation to the meanings and perspectives previously discussed, it is important to keep in mind that definitions and metrics are not necessarily wrong just because they differ; a metric measures what it measures, and while arguments can be made that different definitions or conceptualizations could or should be used to measure global happiness, this does not mean that the way they go about it is inherently wrong or inaccurate. It does, however, give us something to keep in mind when considering the results, and trying to figure out additional reasons why some places differ in their ratings of happiness.

Though there are likely many metrics which could be explored in this brief discussion, we will focus on the World Happiness Report here. The World Happiness Report examines happiness by measuring subjective well-being ("Happiness, trust, and deaths under COVID-19," 2021). Though a number of factors are incorporated and used to break down the scores given to each nation, the main focuses of the World Happiness Report are people's life evaluations, ratings of positive emotions, and ratings of negative emotions, all of which are gathered through the Gallup World Poll surveys ("FAQ," n.d.). As one may notice, this is a noticeably, albeit arguably understandably, Western conceptualization for happiness, since the focus is largely on positive states (Joshanloo, 2014), though in theory the questions regarding life evaluations could allow for a slightly wider variety of views on happiness. Now, though the World Happiness Report is published by the UN, the reason it is an understandably Western view of happiness is because, for better or worse, many studies and fields are rooted in Western lines of thought, resulting in this to be emphasized, even though it is not necessarily representative (Joshanloo).

Looking at the results of the 2021 report, we find that all of the nations ranked in the top 10 for happiness, based "only on the average life evaluations reported by respondents in the Gallup surveys" ("Happiness, trust, and deaths under COVID-19"), are Western, as well as the next 10 besides Israel, which ranked at number 12. If one were to continue down the list, it would be noticeable that though not every Western nation is ranked happier than Eastern counterparts, many of the nations ranked the happiest are Western countries. Given the past several discussions though, hopefully this finding does not come as so great a surprise; though intuitively reasonable to ask people about positive and negative emotions in order to gauge happiness, negative emotions are valued by some as just important as positive ones when it comes to living a happy and good life, as was shown through our explorations of the major Eastern influences on happiness. Accordingly, if negative emotions are used to take away from a person's reported happiness, it is likely that they may end up being ranked as less happy or worse off than they would consider themselves, since the experience of negative emotions is not considered as bad of a thing.

Of course, with all this said, this is a very surface level discussion of the metrics used in the World Happiness Report, and though they are certainly not perfect, they still provide a baseline measure of happiness able to see if nations are doing well or not on average. Hopefully these considerations provide something to think about when looking at results like these, since it is no easy task to get perfectly accurate measurements of a concept that is not viewed the same way by everyone as those measuring it.

With that, our discussions of cultural variations in the meaning and perception of happiness is done. The East and West each have unique histories which have led to the varied and divergent views of happiness we can see today. Though broad differences can be identified when comparing the East and West, it is important to remember that there are not only wide variations within each of them, but also great similarities across the two in both their historical and contemporary views. Going forward, the focus of the discussion will move away from exploring cultural differences regarding happiness, and instead explore other aspects of happiness as well as related topics. This begins in the next chapter with an exploration of subjective well-being.

# Chapter 5: The Science of Subjective Well-being

*"Happiness, not money or prestige, should be regarded as the ultimate currency - the currency by which we take measure of our lives."*
                                  - Tal Ben-Shahar

There are over a dozen journals dedicated to the study of happiness and well-being. While happiness has been studied for hundreds of years, the systematic analysis of subjective well-being is relatively recent. Well-being includes income, personality, age, gender, race, employment, education, religion, marriage, and family. There are several benefits to understanding subjective well-being. Moreover, for those who study happiness, subjective well-being (SWB) is the preferred term. While the science of subjective well-being is organized on core theoretical components, overall life satisfaction is typically measured using self-report surveys and is considered the standard measure of happiness. While in practice, well-being research focuses mainly on an overall measure of well-being, or short measures for quality of life or satisfaction with life (Bartel, 2015). Happiness science is primarily concerned with whether happiness as a state is functional, dysfunctional or neutral ineffective functioning (Diener, 2009, p.3). Theories ask whether happiness is a product of the mind or some external force. Further researchers studying subjective well-being define core elements, creating foundational research. Therefore, a sound base provides some much-needed continuity to research on subjective well-being.

Well-being scholar Edward Diener of the Universities of Utah and Virginia is a leading researcher in the study of happiness. He explains, "subjective well-being (SWB) is the scientific term for happiness and life satisfaction—thinking and feeling that your life is going well, not badly" (2021, np). Core theoretical questions asked by the science of well-being wonder whether internal or external factors shape happiness and whether happiness is an absolute or relative state. Further, the research aims to understand how life can influence SWB. (Diener, 2009,p. 31). Interior locus of origin suggests focusing on inner experiences such as attitude and temperament to provide a more comprehensive well-being image. Therefore psychology as a discipline tends to be more concerned with internal theories.

In contrast, external influences, including income and social status, are likely to be the interests of social scientists, particularly economists and sociologists. Happiness scholars may agree that there are internal and external factors shaping happiness. However, they may disagree over which factor is more significant in the development, and consequently the understanding, of happiness (Diener, 2009, p.3.). On the other hand, an absolute state depends on what other people possess, whereas a relative state is based on standards researchers believe all people use when judging and reacting to life. Diener argues that both absolute and relative factors are significant in understanding well-being (p. 3). In well-being, research theories tend to overlap.

There are variations to the definition of well-being. Diener (2021) explains that subjective well-being distinguishes three forms of happiness: high life satisfaction, frequent positive feeling, and the infrequent negative feeling. High life satisfaction is simply the overall feeling that life is excellent. Individuals who experience high life satisfaction are satisfied with life. They may have a good income and high self-esteem, allowing them to achieve their goals quickly—the second type of happiness is positive feelings distinguished by emotions, like love and enjoyment. Positive feelings are caused by a supportive social network, interest in work or hobbies, and an extroverted personality. Finally, happiness can be characterized as having low negative feelings. People in this category do not experience chronic worry, anger or sadness, likely caused by a low degree of neuroticism. A positive outlook and the ability to match goals to expectations also contribute to low negative feelings. There are different types and different causes of happiness for each individual. Thus Diener argues that the idea that there is a key to happiness is somewhat of a reduction in that people can experience all elements simultaneously.

As mentioned, SWB is dependent on internal factors. The four internal causes of well-being, one being inborn temperament, are what Diener refers to as a top-down influence on well-being (Diener, 2009, p42). Much of what is known about well-being comes from a personality construct. In other words, scientists use personality theory to explain happiness. Thus it makes sense that scientists would concern themselves with research on factors such as neuroticism and extraversion. Research on twins raised in entirely different environments is used to evaluate whether specific traits are inherent or influenced by environmental factors. Thus, research conducted on more than 30,000 twins reported a weighted average heritability of 0.40 for well-being (Røysamb et al., 2018). Heritability is a measurement of the impact of genetics on personality traits on a scale from 0-1. A heritability of

0.40 demonstrates the significance of genetics in well-being. Internal causes of happiness include individual inborn temperament (Diener, 2021). Twin studies demonstrate that twins raised apart tend to have similar levels of subjective well-being.

Personality is an influence on happiness that is both inherent and learned. Outlook and resilience are the last of the four elements. Individual outlook is essential when studying the internal influence on well-being. Cultural perspectives may be primarily optimistic or pessimistic, influencing personal views of life. Further, researching personal outlook as an influence on happiness is interesting as people hold different habits of noticing good things or interpreting ambiguous events positively. Resilience is the ability to navigate and recover from adverse life experiences, and happy people tend to have a high degree. Resilient people do not dwell on adverse events. Instead, they process and let go. While there is happiness scholarly that argues that internal forces undeniably play a role, the external or bottom-up causes of happiness have the most profound influence on the experience of subjective well-being.

In addition to asking where happiness begins and what it depends on, researchers also wonder to what degree happiness is a learned behaviour based on the goals and values of the culture and the surrounding individuals. External factors in subjective well-being are as influential in overall individual happiness as the internal. In other words, people can be happy or unhappy because of personal outlook or mental conditions such as anxiety or depression. Access to sufficient material resources, such as the money to meet basic needs and the ability to fulfill life goals, is one of three external determinants of well-being outlined in the following paragraphs. While seemingly obvious, the science of subjective well-being specifies that people can be unhappy because they do not have access to affordable food and water. This is an essential fact to consider when addressing the impact of the long-term water crisis imposed on many indigenous communities in Canada (Human Rights Watch, 2016, Canada, 2021).

Sufficient social resources and a desirable society are additional bottom-up influences on SWB. First, sufficient social resources demonstrate the difference in social contact but understanding everyone requires some degree of trust and support from others. Further, family, friends and a life partner are critical external causes of well-being, and one or all three are essential to be content. Last, the point that a desirable society will provide for well-being is somewhat apparent. Nevertheless, a society free of war, famine, corruption, and poverty will not negatively affect happiness. Overall, trust in government and a society where people want to help each other has a vital role in individual happiness. In addition to the previously mentioned internal and external factors, Diener argues that well-being research is most interested in economic factors of subjective well-being.

The influence money has on well-being is discussed in detail throughout this book. Therefore we will touch on the impact of money on subjective well-being. According to Diener (2021), money has a vital role to play in life satisfaction. Research on wealthy nations has shown higher than average life satisfaction when compared to developing nations. Specifically, Diener and Seligman (2009) illustrate a correlation ranging from 0.50-0.70 between average well-being and average per capita income across nations. While the correlations mean that wealthy nations are happier than less wealthy nations, they drop substantially when factors such as the quality of government are controlled (p. 209). While using money to measure well-being is exact in that it has an exceptional internal validity, it lacks external validity because it excludes developing nations. Besides, Lucas and Diener (2009) found that income only has about a 5% variance of happiness, but as mentioned, the statistics hide the fact that wealthy people are considerably happier than those who live at the poverty level or below (p. 95). Research by Diener and Seligman (2009) suggests that "losing income may have a more significant influence on well-being than gaining income does (p. 210). Further, the longitudinal data demonstrated that a reason for the correlation between income and well-being is that well-being produces higher incomes rather than the other way around.

Some may wonder, what difference does high subjective well-being make? Very little research was found in the literature on this question. Diener (2021) describes health and longevity, positive social relationships, increased productivity and more excellent citizenship as benefits of high subjective well-being. Individuals who are happy and optimistic have stronger immune systems and are less likely to experience heart disease. Further, happy people are more likely to take care and caution with themselves, such as wearing a seat belt or practicing safe sex. Thus it makes sense that happy people experience healthier and longer lives. Further, the social relationships of happy people are more stable and rewarding. Happy people are likeable, get divorced less and are less likely to be fired. Coupled with the fact that happy people are more likely to receive and give support, it is no doubt that being happy contributes to a cycle of well-being. One interesting finding is that productivity is linked to higher subjective well-being, and happy people are much more likely to help others by donating time or money.

Diener outlines what he perceives as strengths and weaknesses in the field of subjective well-being. Thus according to Diener, the field is unique in that the strengths are often the weaknesses and vice versa. For example, Diener explains that subjective well-being is highly interdisciplinary. This is a strength in that the research has the privilege of receiving multiple perspectives. However, many perspectives are not always positive. Specifically, subjective well-being is rarely a core focus of academic and scientific research due to its highly interdisciplinary nature.

Further, Diener argues there is a lack of funding which inevitably results in a lack of attention from researchers. Further, because there are varying disciplines offering insight, the researchers are often unaware of the work done by other disciplines. A further strength that is also a weakness is that well-being has a strong base in survey sciences such as sociology. Diener maintains that the science of subjective well-being has a strong foundation in survey sciences and roots in the intense focus on individual internal psychological dynamics. Nevertheless, the challenge is similar to the challenge with the interdisciplinary nature of science. Researchers do not share their findings. Thus, academics share well-being discoveries in separate academic journals and tend to ignore each other's findings, resulting in gaps and inconsistencies in what is available. The lack of communication and shared knowledge amongst disciplines is particularly relevant for the last weakness/

strength combo when researching subjective well-being. Diener emphasizes that journalists are interested in the research because happiness research is of particular interest to the general public (p.5).

Consequently, journalists contact well-being researchers, and while sharing knowledge with the public is often a critical goal in any research, data is easily misunderstood or reframed. In support, Diener emphasizes that "most conclusions (on subjective well-being) are tentative and circumscribed" (p.5). In sum, the science on subjective well-being is not complete, and data is best regarded with care, particularly in cases where the status of the research is unclear.

Even though there are limitations, the science of subjective well-being is ongoing. Researchers publish new work often, and information is abundant, notwithstanding any arguments by scholars. In the following chapters, the science of subjective well-being is demonstrated through the lens of various scholarly disciplines. Further, while the following chapters are framed from a specific academic perspective, outside disciplines are included as a way to step away from the lack of shared knowledge in the domain of subjective well-being.

# Chapter 6: Sociology of Well-being

*"When I was in grade school, they told me to write down what I wanted to be when I grew up. I wrote down 'happy'. They told me I didn't understand the assignment, I told them they didn't understand life"*
- Anonymous

Many of us have likely had a similar experience. As a child, "happy" was not considered a future aspiration. In fact, we are expected to decide on whom we want to be, rather than how we want to feel. Although, this may be a profound sentiment to the state of western societies. For many, particularly individuals with status, education and wealth, happiness is assumed. In other words, happiness is a given, and those unhappy may be considered mentally ill or ungrateful. A lack of weight on well-being is a possible reflection of the stigmatization surrounding mental health. The understanding is that happiness is the default, and if it is for some reason not, a person should appear happy nevertheless. According to psychologist and professor James B Allen, happiness is the conscious assessment one makes about their general long-term well-being, and often researchers use these terms interchangeably (Allen, 2018).

It is undoubted there is more to understanding happiness. In a world driven by material gain, a desire to be happy may feel insignificant. Furthermore, it may be challenging to focus on the joy around us because of the seemingly never-ending conveyor belt of 'bad news'. Whether it be a deadly virus, tropical storm, or politician, a definition other than "not feeling bad" seems redundant. Nevertheless, happiness is more than a simple feeling. As a matter of fact, research on happiness recurrently demonstrates the complexities of what is typically understood as mere emotion.

The sociology discipline would be well suited to push for greater attention on the pursuit of well-being; not to satisfy scientific curiosity, but to pay mind to the psychological state of social researchers. Derné (2016) contends studying suffering must contribute to the suffering of scholars, which undoubtedly limits what they can recognize. Fortuitously, social research is easily collected from similar disciplines. Thus, happiness is best understood as interdisciplinary. In other words, experts from various academic disciplines do separate research using their own theoretical approach. Happiness and subjective well-being, often used interchangeably in scholarly research, are well covered in economic and psychological research, which primarily lend to the sociological study of well-being.

According to Ruut Veenhoven, Dutch sociologist and a leader in the sociological study of happiness, the sensation is "a subjective appreciation of life by an individual"(Veenhoven, 2020, p.2). Thus according to Veenhoven, there is no objective standard for happiness. In other words, if a person thinks they are happy, they are, even if they are in a situation considered unpleasant by any other standard. When defining well-being, Veenhoven distinguishes between cognitive and affective appraisals of life (Veenhoven, 2008, p.45). Further, Veenhovens' findings show that life satisfaction is an overall judgment that draws on two sources of information, cognitive and affective. First, a cognitive comparison is made to one's standards of a good life. Essentially, social scientists researching well-being wonder if individuals are content with their life. Second, practical information is gathered from how one feels most of the time, known as the hedonic level of affect or affect theory (Veenhoven, 2006). Veenhoven quotes his 1984 paper, "overall happiness is synonymous with life satisfaction and subjective well-being." Moreover, in a sociological context, happiness is a way to measure life satisfaction throughout a lifetime, including the past and any life events. Thus happiness is not merely a momentary sensation but a collective assessment of overall well-being. Veenhooven believes he can explain why there is a lack of sociological research on well-being and happiness. According to Veenhoven in the 2008 paper Sociological Theories of Subjective Well-being, "subjective well-being is no great issue to sociology" ( p. 44). In other words, the discipline is not interested in the study of well-being. Veenhoven argues that there are pragmatic, ideological and theoretical explanations for the lack of sociological attention to the study of happiness (p.44).

Veenhoven contends that sociologists focus on what people do rather than a sensible theoretical explanation. The primary goal of sociology is to explain social behaviour. In sociology, subjective well-being and happiness are variables in understanding collectivities, whereas subjective well-being inherently focuses on the individual level (p.44). He argues that sociology has considered the objectively harmful elements of social life considerably more pressing and prioritized such studies. Undoubtedly, sociology is primarily focused on collectivity, which has delayed interest in the study of well-being. Therefore, it does appear that when sociology is looking at subjective well-being, it is likely because they were first looking at social problems or the undesirable elements of society (Veenhoven, 2008, p. 44).

Secondly, Veenhoven argues that ideologies inherent to sociology have limited the exploration of well-being. He believes sociologists are not necessarily concerned with how people feel and instead ignore research that contradicts their views (p. 44). For example, people may feel subjectively good in an objectively bad situation, such as happiness, despite living in poverty. Sociology often explains the discrepancy as desirability bias or false consciousness. Last, Veenhoven brazenly argues that subjective well-being is considered by sociology as nothing more than an idea that depends on social comparison with variable standards. He contends that sociology views happiness as a "whimsical state of mind," not necessarily worth pursuing, and hence, not worth studying. However, there are well-known sociological topics that look at well-being, such as the sociology of work and well-being, which often measures life satisfaction. Further, marital satisfaction is commonly measured in family research (p. 44).

The Erasmus Happiness Economics Research Organization is directed by Veenhoven based in the Netherlands and established the World Database of Happiness (WDH), which contains the most comprehensive collections on happiness research. According to the database, overall happiness is "the degree to which an individual judges the overall quality of their life as-a-whole favourable (Veenhoven, 2019). In other words, the Erasmus Happiness Economics Research Organization scientists simply wonder, do you enjoy life? Hence, to make up for the lack of sociological influence in understanding happiness, Veenhoven and his associates contribute considerably to the sociology of happiness. In his article titled Sociology's Blind Eye for Happiness, Veenhoven presents research other sociologists overlook. He argues that a lack of interest in happiness research may be due to sociology's inherent desire to investigate misfortune. Even so, this argument does not consider the relative weight of negative life experiences compared to positive life events. Events that are perceived as negative have a greater impact on an individual than positively perceived events. This is demonstrated by research on impression formation and what is termed the positive-negative asymmetry effect. The findings suggest that "negative information receives more processing and contributes more strongly to the final impression than does positive information" (Baumeister et al., 2001, 323-324). For example, learning something bad about a new business partner will make much more of an impression than learning something good. Consequently, it makes sense that sociology, the study of social life, institutions and phenomena, would begin with the objectively bad aspects of human existence.

Research conducted by Veenhoven offers five findings on happiness research he contends are often overlooked in sociology. Undoubtedly alarming to some, most people are ordinarily happy. This is to say, in survey questions about life satisfaction and daily mood, people generally reported feeling happy. According to empirical research on happiness, on a scale from 1-10, the world average happiness sits around 5.9 (Veenhoven 2014, p.4). Second, a finding often overlooked in sociology is that the average world happiness is on the rise. In other words, researchers have performed periodic assessments of world happiness, and there has been a steady increase in overall global life satisfaction since the 1970s.

However, Veenhoven (2014) found aspects of society that appear to be unrelated to average happiness, such as income inequality and state welfare effort (p. 2). Further findings suggest global inequality in happiness is decreasing (p. 2). A global decrease in happiness inequality means that happiness is felt by wider populations rather than isolated to areas of higher socioeconomic status. Once upon a time, it was believed that the only people who were truly happy were healthy and wealthy, as this is the westernized version of well-being. However, as we hope it is evident throughout this book, happiness can not be defined by mere ethnocentric materialistic standards. Simply, money does not always buy happiness. Comparatively, findings from Matthew A. Killingsworth (2021) mentioned in Chapter 1 suggest that financial income can positively influence overall well-being. Killingsworth sought to assess whether happiness does, in fact, plateau after a household income of $75,000. The data demonstrates that money on its own is nearly unrelated to experienced well-being. In that way, whether participants thought money was important has little significance. Instead, people who are low income are happier if they believe money is not important, whereas those who are high income are happier if they believe money is important (Killingsworth, p. 4). Specifically, participants were asked the question, "To what extent do you think money is indicative of success in life?" The findings demonstrated that income influences those who maintain that being wealthy is the key to success. Killingsworth reports, "the more people equated money and success, the lower their experienced well-being was on average, and there did not appear to be any income level at which equating money and success was associated with greater experienced well-being" (p. 4). Thus, while money may contribute to overall well-being, those who consider money the key to success should prepare for some disappointment.

Further, it is worth noting that the researchers obtained a sample from the United States. Therefore assuming the well-being and income are positively correlated worldwide is ethnocentric, and the data does not represent countries in the global south (i.e. developing countries). Ethnocentric being the evaluation of other cultures based on the standards of one's own. That being the case, the findings that happiness does not plateau after $75,000 may be expressly relevant for those in the United States, the findings may not be generalizable on a global scale. In other words, money does not have the same impact on every culture.

Evidence from Vanhooven (2014) found that the nature of society has a measurable impact on the happiness of society (p.2). Specifically, average happiness varies depending on what type of society is reporting. When Veenhoven says "type of society," what is meant is whether the social and political structure positively impacts the nation. The findings in the world database show a massive variation in the score. For instance, the World Database of Happiness report from 2010 - 2019 found Canada at an average happiness rating of 7.9, which is substantially higher than the average score of 3.8 from Tanzania (Veenhoven, 2019). Thus Veenhoven (2014) argues "happiness is systematically higher in nations that combine a good material standard of living with good governance, freedom. and a climate of tolerance" (p.3) In other words, there is a connection between happiness and whether the government is working for the citizens' best interest. The findings suggest overall happiness can be linked to economic growth, which completely contradicts the Easterlin paradox. A theory published by Richard A. Easterlin in the 1970s suggested economic growth does not improve well-being. For more on the economics of well-being, look to chapter 7.

The position that economic growth and happiness are linked contradicts the research of Steve Derné. Derné is the author of Sociology of Well-being: Lessons From India (2016), an in-depth study of how 203 Indian individuals understand well-being and define a good life. According to his findings, well-being depends not on circumstances or individual traits. Instead, well-being relies solely on one's ability to find meaning and day-to-day pleasures in life.

From the "Sociology of Well-being" Derné (2016) interviewed 65-year-old Armaan Singh, who contemplated suicide when his son died:

> "Armaan Singh talks of health, wealth, and connections to others—what he calls "fame" or shoharat—as necessary to well-being. For Armaan, individual achievements, such as his sporting triumph celebrated at an assembly, are a source of well-being, too. After floundering when his son died, Armaan eventually found a mental approach to facing the trauma, learning from a guru who helped him understand that really the body is nothing. Echoing the Gita, but not quoting it, this unobservant Sikh says one must keep on working without any expectations of the fruits; that one can't change one's circumstances but can change how one thinks about one's circumstances. By seeing happiness as inner, recognizing one can't change one's circumstances, and recognizing that ultimately the body

> *is nothing, Armaan transcends the despair he felt at his son's death. Armaan has pleasures that allow him to continue living with joie de vivre. He watches cricket and cinema with friends, enjoys morning walks and delicious food, gets a thrill from his motorcycle and pretends to flirt with the girls who call him Uncle. By keeping a positive outlook, Armaan enjoys felicitous interactions with everyone around him: "If you're good, everybody is good; if you're happy, everybody is happy."*

Derné (2016) explains when Armaan placed effort into relationships that create a chain of well-being that extends beyond himself and back to himself, he changed his well-being from a purely internal event to include an external contribution to his well-being. Thus the perspective offered by Derné is that well-being comes from how people think about their situations. Happiness does not stem from circumstance or a situation. Of course, people need to have their basic needs met, health, social and financial. Derné uses the term modicum to describe the degree to which needs must be met. In other words, having very little income, poor health, unstable social connections and poor opportunities do not mean one automatically has poor well-being. All in all, how people perceive their income, health, connections, and opportunities is essential to their overall well-being.

Two of the Indian citizens interviewed by Derné (2016) were noted to be in poor health and remain neglected by their families. Seventynine-year-old Prakash Tyagi and 80-year-old Ishwar Kumar shared similar experiences. Yet, Ishwar is bitter while Prakash continues to report well-being by focusing on how he "can still walk, and how every day offers a new elegance." Derné ultimately demonstrated how pleasant ritual activities, feeling connected to one another, and having meaningful ways to navigate difficult life situations are why religion is often associated with greater well-being. Moreover, the interviews provide the conclusion that external situations have little to do with well-being.

Notwithstanding the relatively small body of sociology conducted on well-being, the research does suggest it is much more complex than a simple emotion. A greater focus on qualitative research could produce compelling findings that address individual experience. Qualitative research is research based on first-hand human experience gathered through surveys and questionnaires in contrast to quantitative research, in which the research is focused on collecting and analyzing data. Qualitative research is uniquely suited for happiness research in that individuals are not a number. Instead, the questions are often open-ended to fully grasp the experience of the subject.

While the argument by Veenhoven introduced at the beginning of this chapter that sociologists do not consider well-being in their research has some truth, today happiness data is growing mainly in part due to the research of sociologists like Vanhooven and Derné who, with the individuals at the core, provide an understanding of happiness through the eyes of the people. As suggested before, research on well-being that contains primarily multiple-choice surveys and studying numbers does not provide the same insight into well-being as an in-depth interview. While the study of well-being is growing in sociology, economic and psychological perspectives paved the way. Qualitative research on the sociology of subjective well-being cross-culturally would be a fruitful area for further work.

# Chapter 7: Economics of Happiness

*"Money, it's a crime. Share it fairly but don't take a slice of my pie. Money, so they say, is the root of all evil today"*
*- Pink Floyd 1981*

There is a great deal of emphasis on financial wealth and stability in modern society. To be happy is to have an objectively large dollar amount sitting in the bank. Further, happiness is connected to the security money provides. The media, government policy, and institutional goals distort the importance of money and its ability to contribute to well-being. Financial standing is a primary indicator of overall well-being and quality of life by each; thus, it makes sense that people are drawn to wealth. Entire news segments and papers are dedicated to reporting economic issues, the stock market and financial advice. Politicians are expected to address budgets and the economy (Diener & Seligman, 2004). Therefore, despite how hard we try, economic well-being will never depend entirely on a high income.

There is no denying that money makes life easier. Individuals who can afford a chauffeur, delivery service, live-in chef, security, and private healthcare experience a higher quality of well-being than a single unemployed individual. In 2018, author and researcher Shailja Patel addressed just how much difference money can make in daily life. Patel describes the people who claim "everyone has the same 24 hours" as speaking from a place of privilege. She argues that those with a private jet or a vehicle of any sort do not have the same 24 hours as a person who uses public transit or is forced to walk. She claims that money buys time and privilege. Of course, income is a fair measurement of happiness for those who have it. It is undeniable that money provides access, but economic well-being is about so much more than primo healthcare.

The economics of happiness is a social science focused on how participation in the production, distribution and access to goods and services include overall subjective well-being (SWB). Mariano Rojas (2019), author of The Economics of Happiness, argues that the first scholars interested in the study of happiness were not interested in the individual assessment of happiness. Instead, there was a focus on defining happiness. Philosopher Jeremey Bentham outlined in 1781 a theory of happiness and action. Essentially the principle argues that happiness can be measured. Specifically, an action is assessed according to how much happiness it produces (Fox, 2012). Bentham's philosophy spread and economists incorporated elements of the concept (more on utilitarianism, see Chapter 1). The individual experience grew irrelevant as happiness became an academic construct rather than a result of personal experiences. Economics experts became attuned to the fact that happiness is more than positive emotions. Happiness and the overall experience of well-being affect human behaviour and can be linked to motivation and productivity (Rojas, p. 8). Nevertheless, philosophers and social scientists continued to debate about happiness in both experience and theory.

During the early twentieth century, the Gross Domestic Product (GDP), a national accounting system, was developed to measure the collective income of societies. The GDP eventually became a significant indicator of the progress and development of a nation. Gross Domestic Product (GDP) is an estimate of the economic standing of a nation. GDP is measured by adding a nation's personal consumption expenditures, government expenditures, net exports and net capital. In other words, data is collected by adding how much the public spends on goods and services, infrastructure, debt, exports' value, and the increase in a national total potential income from monetized goods (Costanza et al. 2014). Robert Costanza, Maureen Hart, Ida Kubiszewski and John Talberth, authors of the article A Short History of GDP: Moving Towards Better Measures of Human Well-being, argue that the GDP is misused as a measure of national well-being. Constanza et al. (2014) explain that any economist familiar with GDP will stress that the analysis of Gross Domestic Product is a tool to measure economic activity and is ineffective when measuring economic and social well-being. (p. 91).

Rojas (2019) explains that economics began as the study of prices, quantities and markets. However, as the study moved into the mid-twentieth century, they understood they were approaching ingredients to human happiness. That is to say, economists learned that happiness motivates human behaviour and can explain prices and support most economic decisions (p. 8). It seems GDP is useful for understanding human happiness when looking at a capitalist economy. In Canada, the National Gross Domestic Product by income and expenditure is at the centre of macroeconomic analysis and policy-making (Statistics Canada, 2021). A focus on the consumption of goods as an indicator of well-being does not recognize families without access to essential goods and services, let alone entire regions. Some argue for the abandonment of GDP as a typical measurement of happiness entirely. Several researchers agree that there are more suitable alternatives when researching economics and happiness (Dick 2019; Rojas 2019; Costanza et al., 2014). Rojas explains that economists assumed a higher income made it easier for people to meet their needs, ultimately leading to greater well-being. In contrast, Diener and Seligman (2004) argue in Beyond Money: Toward an Economy of Well-Being, that "money is a means to an end, and that end is well-being" (p. 2). They go on to explain that economic prosperity does not, however, guarantee happiness.

Although GDP is used to understand national well-being, it primarily measures "monetary transactions related to producing goods and services" (Costanza et al., 2014, p. 93). GDP overlooks aspects of society relevant when researching the economics of well-being, such as unequal wealth distribution and economic welfare. Consequently, a measurement of economic well-being such as GDP is based on increased jobs, income and other basic needs, which is not an assessment of well-being. Economists are better suited to look beyond GDP for insight into well-being. Nevertheless, there is an undeniable relationship between national well-being and economic prosperity. In a report in 2004, there was a substantial correlation (0.50-0.70) between average well-being and average per capita income (Diener & Seligman, 2004, p.5). Although, the research does not explain precisely what economic prosperity contributes to well-being. An essential point is made by Costanza et al. in that the economics of well-being neglects to acknowledge degrees of poverty (p. 94). They stress that science must recognize the difference between absolute poverty in terms of low quality of life rather than poverty in terms of solely low financial income (p. 94). While the above research does demonstrate an impressive correlation, there is undeniable evidence demonstrating that financial well-being beyond a certain level does not replace healthy relationships, connections with nature, and other dimensions of human happiness (Costanza et al. 2014; Michalos et al. 2009).

Several alternative methods have been proposed to measure economic well-being. An improvement to the GDP being Human Development Index (HDI), which is a multidimensional approach used by policymakers to measure three critical dimensions of human development published by the United Nations Development Programme (Yang, 2018). Researchers Roser (2019) and Hou et al. (2015) explain that the core elements of human development under the HDI are a long and healthy life, access to education, and a decent standard of living. Nevertheless, there are notable concerns with the HDI, particularly when measuring well-being. Hou et al. (2015) address methodological and dimensional issues with the HDI in the article The Dynamics of the Human Development Index, where they offer the HDIF as a more accurate demonstration of a country's development. The study argues that life expectancy is not suitable for comparing health changes between countries at different income levels and different points in time.

On the other hand, the HDIF assesses under-five mortality rates rather than life expectancy. Infant mortality rates can be helpful to study overall subjective well-being. Notably, the life expectancy of children under five is a strong indicator of a nation's economic, environmental and social conditions (WHO, 2021). As outlined, attention to distinct elements of human development is fundamental when researching the economic well-being of a society, particularly those with vulnerable populations. The HDI is an improvement to the GDP in that it includes elements other than financial indicators. Moreover, the research demonstrates that the HDIF allows policymakers to measure the efficacy of their policies and make adjustments, which is paramount for developing nations (Hou et al., 2015).

Research demonstrates that an accurate measurement of well-being using GDP is trivial, and the HDI is widely scrutinized (Yang, 2018); Therefore, alternatives such as the Global Prosperity Index (GPI) provide insight into how prosperity is forming and changing across the globe (Legatum Institute, 2020). Each year since 2007, the private Legatum Institute has published a GPI that uses a wide variety of previously unrecognized indicators in combination with economic factors (Fox, 2012). First and foremost, the GPI is based on data that is both public and verifiable. Moreover, the index consists of 12 pillars of prosperity such as health, education and social capital, and 66 elements within the pillars. The elements represent key policy areas, such as government integrity and air pollution, and were created to encourage and support more focused action (Legatum Institute, 2020). There are many ways the GPI is a vast improvement from the GDP, one such being a weak performance in a pillar can indicate where a country needs attention. Therefore, researchers can identify what policy-related factor is fuelling the trend. For example, findings may show that poor prosperity is linked to poor working conditions.

Consequently, the index could review what unfair labour laws are driving a weak performance. This information can allow policymakers to look toward specific areas that need improvement. Therefore, GPI is a measurement of economic well-being, including financial status and emphasizes how economic standing is connected to fundamental elements of human well-being. To elaborate on the 66 elements, each outlines components of a society that contribute to well-being. Specifically, one pillar measured by the index is social capital. Social capital is the social cohesion of a society. The report indicates that "a person's well-being is best provided for in a society where people trust one another and have the support of their friends and family" (Legatum Institute, 2020, p. 25). The specific elements of social capital measured by the GPI can be easily linked to well-being. Personal and family relationships, the strength of social networks, civic and social participation and institutional trust, contribute to social capital. Lower levels of institutional trust are linked to slower economic growth and social well-being. Thus, social capital demonstrates the importance of social networks in economic growth as well as SWB.

It is only since the work of Richard Easterlin in the mid-1970's that the importance of individual subjectivity was identified in the study of happiness. Thus for the first time, shifting the economics of happiness from the study of objects to people. Easterlin began to research the connection between economics and happiness by abandoning preconceived notions and ethical and moral considerations (Rojas, 2019, p.4). Instead, he turned to research and found that despite the growing American economy, the country's overall well-being remained the same. (ESRC, 2021). Rojas argues Easterlin's discovery "shifted economics away from the path of uncorroborated presumptions as well as from relying on ethical and doctrinal considerations to address well-being issues" (p. 5). In other words, Easterlin challenged economics to move away from generalization and assumptions about happiness. Not only did he incorporate methods unique to the study of the economics of happiness. Nevertheless, the method recognized happiness as people's experience rather than a construct created by social scientists.

Furthermore, Easterlin emphasized the fact that individuals are the authority in their life rather than relying on the perspective of scholars. While Easterlin first published findings in 1995 on the United States, he gradually included Japan and nine other developed nations. The findings (which he refers to as the happiness-income paradox), discovered across a wide range of countries, rich and poor, ex-communist and capitalist, across five continents, a higher rate of economic growth does not result in a more significant increase of happiness (Easterlin et al. 2010, p. 22466). Easterlin et al. revisited the happiness-income paradox or the Easterlin Paradox in 2010, with the addition of 17 Latin American countries, 17 developed countries, and 11 Eastern European countries recently transitioned from socialism to capitalism and nine less developed countries across Asia, Latin America, and Africa. In order to collect data, the Easterlin Paradox explains happiness in terms of life satisfaction and financial satisfaction. Specifically, for a worldwide sample of 37 countries for 12 to 34 years, there is no significant relationship between improved life satisfaction and economic growth. No significant relationship is not to say some countries do not display a greater connection between well-being and economic growth than others, as is demonstrated by the research of Killingsworth mentioned in earlier chapters. Instead, the data suggests the relationship is not significant on a global scale.

The main goal of this chapter is to outline the economic measures of happiness. The result demonstrates that GDP is not a measure of economic well-being that best serves the nation's individuals, but primarily serves the wealthy as a tool to measure success. The relevance of including social, educational and health care elements in the study of economic well-being is supported by the ability of GPI to identify weaknesses within policy. There is, therefore, a need for policymakers to abandon the GDP and instead utilize one of the better options to measure economic well-being and support nations.

# Chapter 8: Social-Scientific Perspectives to Happiness & Positive Psychology

*"Happiness depends more on how life strikes you than on what happens."*
- Unknown

This chapter will specifically provide a scientist-practitioner's approach to understanding happiness.

Happiness is not pragmatically definable when isolated from context. According to the Oxford Dictionary, happiness is defined as "a state of being happy."

A deep-dive into various wings of philosophy and linguistics reveals a glut of polarized, semantical, and often banal definitions of happiness. The diaspora of perspectives is highly attributable to novel philosophies - products of unique time and geography. However, two constants perforate nearly every definition of happiness regardless of the time and place of conception; joy and experience. These aspects of happiness are only constant in their omnipresence, however, the meaning of these constants are as varied as the people, places, and times that defined them. This leads us back to where we started - a pervasive division of global conceptions and definitions of happiness.

Attempting to ascribe a definition to happiness introduces troublesome physical and philosophical paradoxes. Namely, happiness is not necessarily apparent in one's conscious awareness from moment to moment. Several notable scholars and philosophers assert that happiness is only experienced in retrospect, while others attempt to demonstrate that happiness is a byproduct of mindfulness, giving attention to all aspects of the present moment. More divergent perspectives attempt to convey that true happiness cannot be recognized by the conscious mind, and is only felt when one chooses to 'let go' of their conscious thoughts and awarenesses in an attempt to disempower neuroses and cognitive distortion.

For the purposes of this chapter, we will adopt a perception of happiness that is supported by Dr. Martin Seligman throughout his work in the field of positive psychology. This description of happiness is inclusive, well-studied, and relatively equitable to global perspectives about the origins and dynamics of happiness.

Happiness is a frame of reference - a summation that combines all aspects of life and their effects on one's psyche into the context of an individual. To that end, happiness is ultimately relative, and by extension undefinable as a practical entity.

This chapter touches upon psychological perspectives of happiness as approached through a scientist-practitioner model. This includes an exploration of neurophysiological foundations of various aspects of happiness and a brief foray into positive psychology as a novel academic discipline attempting to rework the traditional forms of logos that perpetuate dialogue on happiness.

**Neuroscientific Foundations of Happiness: Hedonia, Eudaimonia, and Beyond**

Among the scientists who advocate on behalf of a model of happiness as an artifact of our conscious awareness are Morten Kringelbach and Kent Berridge. These Danish neuroscientists study the neuroscientific underpinnings of happiness and pleasure. They make a compelling argument that neuroscientific processes associated with happiness are relatively objective, and may be a valuable first-step in approaching the conundrum of defining happiness outside the context of an individual's lived experience.

Kringelbach and Berridge build their case by beginning with two mood-aspects that science allows us to empirically validate with relative reliability; hedonia (pleasure) and eudaimonia (a life well lived). As was discussed in chapters 2 and 3, these aspects of happiness were originally pondered by aristotle. Appropriately, their modern-day translations are essentially 'pleasure' and 'meaning'. More recently, the field of positive psychology has established empirical means of measuring other discrete aspects of happiness that involve engagement, for better or worse, in various lived experiences.

Beginning a neuropsychological foray into happiness with macroscopic components of happiness is an important step; self-report measures that attempt to quantify these variables provide context for further exploration into problems of pleasure, meaning, and engagement at the neurological level. That said, subjective self-report measures are not rigorous enough to provide empirical clarity past the point of discerning if, and why, problems involving happiness may exist in an individual.

*"It is important to note that our focus on the hedonia component of happiness should not be confused with hedonism, which is the pursuit of pleasure for pleasure's own sake, and more akin to the addiction features we describe below. Also, to focus on hedonics does not deny that some ascetics may have found bliss through painful self sacrifice, but simply reflects that positive hedonic tone is indispensable to most people seeking happiness"* (Kringelbach & Berridge, 2009, p.3).

Sigmund Freud is well-known for adopting a tacit, binary approach to understanding the nature of happiness - one that enforces the escape from displeasure and attainment of pleasure as a backbone for establishing a preliminary essence about happiness. This model of happiness is quite consonant from a traditional neuroscientists perspective; studying the physiology of brain substrates associated with pleasure, reward, and drive-behaviours would undoubtedly make the journey into understanding happiness at the brain-behaviour level extremely straightforward. Nevertheless, investing full consideration in this approach would be naive, even in the wake of it's intuitive logic. The question of how meaning and engagement are created by the brain still persists. In sum, pleasure and happiness are not synonymous.

William James (1920) also pursued a binary understanding of happiness through an exclusive focus on eliminating displeasure; "happiness, I have lately discovered, is no positive feeling, but a negative condition of freedom from a number of restrictive sensations of which our organism usually seems the seat. When they are wiped out, the clearness and cleanness of the contrast is happiness. This is why anaesthetics make us so happy. But don't you take to drink on that account."

As mentioned, the problem of constraining happiness within the boundary of positive and negative affect is a lack of consideration for what happiness is; a symphony of circumstances that relies on one's evaluation of events, people, feelings, and more within the context of an individual's life.

The question for neuroscienctists does not exclusively focus on investigating neurological underpinnings of affect (though, that is a crucial component of exploring happiness), but rather how different affect states are balanced in the brain to create conditions that could be extrapolated to be symbolic of 'happiness'. The ethos of this approach relies on understanding that the interaction of affect-states is not merely subjective - they are also represented by physiological processes. Thus, in this context, neurophysiology is able to capture what other fields fundamentally cannot: an objective approach to pragmatically defining happiness through observable means.

It is important to note that affectives states are not the same as conscious affective feelings. Kringelback (2004) notes that conscious affective feelings are the lived-experiences of positive or negative emotions. They ultimately have no objective measure in neurophysiology, and while they may have diffuse effects on observable behaviour, they are otherwise unobservable. In essence, affect itself transcends conscious processes or behavioural reactions - herein lies the utility of distinguishing between affective-states and conscious affective feelings.

## Hedonic Neuroscience

The neurophysiology of pleasure cannot be observed in isolation. Pleasure, in this regard, is a scientific behemoth, a neurological microcosm, an interactive and highly dynamic cacophony of neurological cause-and-effect. To that end, we must understand that pleasure has multiple subtypes. We must also understand that brain substrates, processes, and networks overlap to a significant degree in processing different forms of pleasure. For example, primal pleasures such as eating food are processed in similar brain-structures that process sensory pleasures like massages, or addictive pleasures like drugs or alcohol. Needless to say, the integration of these pleasure-substrates into the rest of the brain is extremely differentiated. The brain, as an interface, is an exponential series of dynamic inputs and outputs from substrates that, in effect, act as their own interfaces - process-specific hubs for connectivity with other hubs. So, while 'pleasure-centres' overlap in their processing, the outcomes of that processing are varied.

> *"Pleasure is never merely a sensation or a thought, but is instead an additional hedonic gloss generated by the brain via dedicated systems" (Frijda, 2010, p.15).*

Pleasure-activated substrates are fairly plentiful within the brain. A colloquial approach to understanding their function may be to envision them 'lighting-up' as a consequence of experiencing pleasure. These often include substrates within the accumbens, cingulate and orbitofrontal cortices, medial PFC, and the brainstem (Smith et al, 2010). While pleasure-reactant brain structures are relatively easy to find, there is disparity in the quantity of pleasure-causing brain structures within the brain - 'liking' mechanisms. These may be referred to as hedonic hotspots, and are typically found in subcortical areas that measure under a cubic centimeter in volume. These tiny hotspots can be found in the ventral pallidum, parabrachial nucleus (within the pons), and deep within limbic cortical regions (Kringelbach & Berridge, 2010).

Hedonic hotspots are not intuitively placed; they can be quite spread-out throughout various structures that are not always well connected. By contrast however, the hotspots themselves are extremely well integrated to one another despite existing in seemingly disparate locations. Their level of integration is evident in a variety of trials wherein microinjections of opiates initiated a cascade of neurochemical reactions across every hotspot. The self-report of subjects' conscious affective feelings were a two-to-three-fold increase in 'liking' a novel taste, smell, or sensation (Robinson and Bemdge, 1993).

Hotspot networks essentially function as a 'circuit' that responds to commands from executive processing substrates most-often found in the neocortex. This hierarchy of command is a cooperative neurological process - hotspots can be seen 'cooperating' to elicit a stronger liking response within executive substrates atop the hierarchy. The executive centres thereby dictate other substrates to act in accordance with the magnitude of the liking response, perhaps by initiating a cascade of drive-behaviours, seeking-behaviour, or showing pleasure or satisfaction through a variety of physiological and behavioural processes. The former, initiation of drive and seeking behaviours, is called incentive salience, or wanting.

Incentive salience (wanting) is not to be confused with liking. As can be seen in contexts of addiction, wanting a reward (often evidenced by drive and seeking behaviours) is sometimes discontinuous with the liking of that reward (often evidenced by dread and anhedonia after receiving the reward). The interaction of profound wanting despite the expectation of anhedonia is a neurological paradox that highlights the limitations and pitfalls of our central nervous system. While wanting processes are mediated by subcortical limbic structures, our centres for planning, cost-response analyses, and foresight are neocortical. The limbic system and neocortex have a complicated relationship that is predisposed by evolutionary discontinuity, mainly the brain-structures evolved in different eras of human evolution, to meet vastly different evolutionary niches. The modern-day product of this discontinuity is a 'push-and-pull' effect between the mesolimbic structures that perpetually 'want', and the neocortical structures that advise. As a result, managing incentive salience through exercises that bolster connectivity between these substrates is a hugely crucial ingredient to happiness. Under regulated 'wanting', through both affective states and conscious affective feelings, without sufficient consultation from our executive neocortex, is deeply caustic to happiness over time.

This information alone does not form a comprehensive model for the neuroscience of happiness. Rather, we must investigate how it relates to the prospective neurology of eudaimonic happiness - the happiness derived from meaning, and meaning derived from happiness. While not conclusively understood, neuroscientists are taking note of a potentially salient starting point; the brain's default mode network. It is proposed by Drevets et al (1997) and

Kringelbach & Berridge (2010) that the default mode network may play an important role in providing a bridge between eudaimonia and hedonia. The orbitofrontal cortex and anterior-cingulate are largely associated in pleasure recognition processes. They also contain substrates that interface with both the brain's default mode network and the hedonic networks (Kringelbach & Berridge, 2010).

Drevetes et al (1997) provided one of the first empirical foundations for the idea that the default mode network could be associated with affect-states and conscious affective thoughts. By observing modulation in the metabolic pathways of the subgenual cingulate cortex and orbitofrontal cortices (frontal networks that form part of the physiological pathway for the default mode network), Drevetes and their colleagues were able to observe affect-state changes in sufferers with pathological forms of anhedonia, like clinical depression and bipolarity-induced depression. The default mode represents a hopeful embark into this murky topic, but there is still a great deal of exploration required to even ascertain the gravity of these preliminary findings and theories:

"Pathological self-representations by the frontal default network could also provide a potential link between hedonic distortions of happiness that are accompanied by eudaimonic dissatisfaction, such as in cognitive rumination of depression. Conversely, mindfulness based cognitive therapy for depression, which aims to disengage from dysphoria-activated depressogenic thinking, might conceivably recruit default network circuitry to help mediate improvement in happiness via a linkage to hedonic circuitry" (Kringelbach & Berridge, 2010, p.9)

The current literature does not support a conclusive understanding of the neurological origins of eudaimonia. Rather, research communities in the social sciences, psychology, psychiatry, and neuroscience support the idea that artifacts of pleasure - by virtue of neurophysiological observation, are involved in creating the brain-based circumstances that invoke eudaimonia in our conscious affective thoughts.

**Final Thoughts on Neuroscience of Happiness**

Despite being preliminary in scope, this chapter's focus is to elucidate the value in exploring happiness in-terms of neurophysiological analogues.

The successful finding and synthesis of our current understandings of neurophysiology in the context of affect-states and conscious affective thoughts is, in large part, owed to the collaborative efforts of interdisciplinary professionals and research bodies. The amelioration of psychological problems delivered by the field of psychology has given rise to one of the most impactful research collaborations in the social sciences - the coordination of psychology, medicine, neuroscience, and other life-sciences to attain a common goal; ameliorate subjective anguish and search for its determinants.

The field of positive psychology ultimately catalyzes this goal into something holistic, rigorous, and equitable to a variety of perspectives on the origins, trends, and fortification of happiness.

## Positive Psychology: Psychology Reborn

If happiness is to be experienced, it cannot be objectified.

Solutions to many of western society's modern-day problems often rely on methodologically manipulating variables to attain a desired outcome. Case and point, if a light-bulb burns out, we may consider buying ourselves a ladder and a pack of new light bulbs from the hardware store. After attaining the required materials, we might erect the ladder, climb toward the dead light bulb, and replace it with a new one. We enact this cadence expecting our problem to be ameliorated; the new bulb is expected to illuminate.

You install the bulb, retract the ladder, and flip the light switch. The new light bulb still does not illuminate. What now? Perhaps after a minute of pondering the problem further, the whole light fixture dies and you are left in the dark. At such a point, we continue to manipulate variables until we receive the desired outcome - perhaps we flip the circuit-breakers, check the amperage of the new bulb, re-solder electrical joints in the light fixture, etc.

There is nothing wrong with this approach assuming that our desired outcome relies on manipulating objects in the physical world. In this example, that is represented by acquiring light by means of fixing electrical components within an electrical circuit. However, applying this approach to the pursuit of happiness introduces a paradox; happiness is immaterial, and without directly adjusting one's neurophysiology, tinkering with elements of the material world will not have a consequential effect on happiness - at least, not within the realm of our previously mentioned definition of happiness; a frame of contextual reference.

For argument's sake, we will recognize that changing physical portions of our environment may ameliorate psychological burdens - perhaps organizing one's bedroom relieves stress, or working out is an effective escape from general anxieties. Lest, as mentioned in the previous section's exploration of the neuroscientific basis of happiness, the absence of psychological burdens is not synonymous with happiness.

Let's not forget, happiness is not exclusively the absence or presence of anything - it is not an entity that can be had, or not had by our culturally ingrained means of pursuit or acquisition. To label it as such reinforces the paradox that keeps it perpetually out of reach - the paradox that motivates us to pursue something that often vanishes if pursued.

To reiterate, from a positive psychological perspective, happiness must only be considered a frame of reference; a colouring of one's outlook that fosters satisfaction without longing or pursuit. This frame of reference organically produces affective byproducts such as gratitude, presence and connectedness, whether consciously or otherwise. Importantly, happiness itself can be bolstered, even invoked through intentional practice of some of the affective states just mentioned. This simple, yet unintuitive finding is a flagship tenant of the positive psychology movement.

Martin Seligman is the founder and champion of the positive psychology movement. In 1998, during his term as president of the American Psychological Association, he coined the term 'positive psychology' to define his presidential focus. Seligman wanted to shift the focus of modern psychology away from the exclusive focus of ameliorating mental suffering. Seligman asserted that the at-times myopic tendencies of modern psychology fell short of delivering the best-care possible, and was ultimately neglectful to important considerations more commonly tended to by practitioners of social psychology, social work, and personal mentorship. As such, Seligman forged a new branch of psychological research that strives to empower patients through the formation of eudaimonia - 'a life well lived'.

Positive psychology was often met with caution and skepticism in its earliest years. The field was criticised for appearing less scientifically rigorous and comprehensive than that of it's cousin branches, such as cognitive psychology, and the then ballooning field of brain-behaviour dynamics. Despite the field's validity being mocked for it's perpetuation of what some called 'sesame-street ethics', Seligman truly defied expectations, eventually starting a graduate research program in positive psychology at the University of Pennsylvania. To this day, the Master of Positive Psychology program remains one of the most competitive and exclusive psychology graduate programs in the world. Seligman himself is among the most influential research psychologists of his time, with over 150 first-author publications and 40,000 collaborative citations. He is also a best selling author thanks to his books 'Authentic Happiness' and 'Flourish'.

Positive psychology is broad, no doubt. This chapter will illustrate one of the most central concepts of the positive psychology methodology - PERMA.

PERMA is a mnemonic that details Seligman's theory of wellbeing. Positive emotions, Engagement, Relationships, Meaning, and Accomplishments. Seligman's research has revealed these areas to be the most important in attaining, and maintaining happiness. He asserts that paying attention to, and pursuing equity in these areas can not only ameliorate psychological anguish, but create circumstances to greatly reduce stress and preserve one's physical longevity as well.

Positive Emotions relate to the affective states and conscious affective thoughts we discussed in the earlier section on the neuroscience of happiness. Finding opportunities to experience positive emotions such as joy, excitement, pride, and satisfaction are crucial to fulfilling the criteria for positive emotions.

Engagement is fairly diverse and contextual insofar as fulfilling it's criteria in the PERMA framework. Essentially, engagement can be summarized by participating in activities, actions, or constructs that one enjoys or finds interesting. Engagement requires cognitive taxation that involves some level of challenge. However challenging the engagement opportunity may be, it must also not deter the participant due to a lack of efficacy. Passion and focus are central tenants to finding opportunities to exercise engagement.

Relationships are exactly that; exploring opportunities to connect with other people. Whether the connection is superficial or deep, Christopher Peterson, cofounder of the positive psychology movement, summarizes the sentiment perfectly: "Other People are the best antidote to the downs of life and the single most reliable up" (Flourish, 2012).

Meaning is another varied and contextual component of Seligman's theory of well-being. An omnipresent attribute of meaning is it's motivational properties, allowing people to 'carry-on' in times of uncertainty. Meaning can also be described as finding the 'why' behind what one does, even if one is faced with circumstances wherein they do not have autonomy, finding a 'why' can be a potent experience in positive perspective building.

Accomplishments involve attaining, and recognizing one's successes - no matter how big or small.

Seligman's positive psychology is not an infallible perspective. It is one of many potent guides that lead people toward eudaimonia - the goal of this text.

# Chapter 9: Becoming Happier - From Theory to Practice

*"We tend to forget that happiness doesn't come as a result of getting something we don't have, but rather of recognizing and appreciating what we do have."*
                                    - Frederick Keonig

In order to attain and maintain happiness as a state of well-being, it is important to take practical action to fulfil this aim in addition to internalizing the content of any given theory of happiness that can help guide decisions and thinking. Thus far we have focused on addressing different theoretical conceptions of happiness in significant variety and depth. Until this point, there has been a gap in our review of happiness as we have discussed merely in passing the practical research-backed methods for enhancing happiness and well-being in our daily lives. The purpose of this chapter is to fill this gap by addressing how readers can better engage in happiness as an activity. In particular, this chapter will address the science of sleep, stress, gratitude, and purpose in relation to happiness.

**Sleep**

A night of rest is foundational to enabling individuals to reach a state of happiness and well-being. Sleep is one of the most important activities that all mammals perform on a daily basis. The importance of sleep is self-evident in that evolution would never select for a massively time-intensive (in that you spend many hours unawake, not producing, and vulnerable to predation) and resource intensive (in that there is significant caloric burn during sleep) process unless it was of very substantial importance.

The American Psychological Association (APA) recognises the importance of sleep to well-being. The APA's review of sleep science led them to conclude that failing to get sufficient sleep can lead to dysfunction in cognition and memory, an abnormally high level of resting stress response, and dysregulation in metabolic activity. Indeed, readers will likely know from personal experience that low-sleep undermines emotional control and stability. Quantitative evidence also establishes that insufficient sleep produces anger as it activates the fight or flight pathways in the brain's amygdala (Saghir et al., 2018).

Just as there is a link between anger and sleep, there is an established link between sleep and happiness. A study in 2018 found that sleep predicts subjective measures of well-being, even after controlling for other variables (Shin & Kim, 2018). As a rough guide, it is important to sleep around eight hours to feel healthy. However, there is more that can go into a night of well-rested sleep besides duration. In particular, sleep scientist Matt Walker suggests ten tips for improving sleep (and thus your general happiness): (1) sleep at a routine and regular time as sleep is not something that can be traded between nights, (2) avoid heavy cardio exercise before bed as this can activate certain pathways in the brain that work to increase wakefulness, (3) avoid the consumption of stimulant or wakefulness drugs such as nicotine, caffeine, and adderall many hours before bedtime, (4) avoid the consumption of drugs like alcohol or sedative drugs as these can disrupt the normal and healthy changing of sleep cycles and leave you waking unrested, (5) avoid eating a heavy meal before sleeping as the energy involved in the digestive process for heavy caloric meals can make sleep less effective, (6) relax, unwind, and meditate before sleeping in order to lower your state of mental activity, (7) have healthy day-night light exposure at proper times of day (eg. avoid staying in a bright artificially lighted environment all day until immediately before sleep), (8) reduce your body temperature before bed by keeping the room temperature on the colder side, (9) remove distractions from your room such as a television or your phone if it is keeping you awake with notifications, and (10) avoid sitting awake in bed if you cannot fall asleep (Masterclass, 2021).

In addition to following these sleep behavioral adjustments, it is also possible to induce sleep via the supplementation of natural compounds available over the counter such as the hormone melatonin. Other sleep enhancement compounds include those used by Stanford neurobiologist Andrew Huberman such as apigen, magnesium threonate, and theanine (Ferriss, 2021). Sleep is directly related to happiness and, thankfully, there is much improvement individuals can achieve to their sleep as a result of relatively simple behavioral modifications.

**Stress**

It is obvious that chronically stressed individuals are likely to be unhappy compared to their less-stressed peers. Stress is an emotion that everyone feels from time to time, irrespective of their place in life. However, stress in the modern era may be particularly problematic. There has been a growing trend of anxiety and stress recorded in population level statistics, especially among the youngest people in the United States. Evidence from the National Survey on Drugs and Health indicated that there was an increase in reported anxiety from approximately 5% in 2008 to 7% in 2018 and 8% to 15% among youth during the same time period (Goodwin et al., 2020). Evidence has looked to establish the connection between stress and unhappiness and found that there is in fact a strong correlation (Schiffrin & Nelson, 2010). In short, happy and healthy people do not lead lives under constant stress.

One method, then, for becoming happier is to follow best practices for stress reduction. There are a wide variety of ways for reducing stress, some of which have received greater scholarly attention than others. One exercise for stress management as a means to increase happiness is guided imagery. This involves taking a kind of pretend vacation in times of stress. For example, this could entail closing your eyes and imagining yourself at a tropical vista complete with envisioning warm sunlight, humid ocean breeze, sweet tropical flowers, and taste of coconut (Kaiser, 2019). Guided imagery exercises of this type have been tested and found effective in clinical trials, such as one study that found 91% of participants reported higher general feelings of well-being as a result of the exercise (Carter, 2006).

Another related option for increasing happiness is meditation. Meditation can be defined as training one's attention to perceive the 'self' behind one's rational and constantly thinking mind. Meditation can produce increased mindfulness (the capacity to live in the moment and observe the world around you in a non-judgemental manner), self-compassion, and happiness (Campos et al., 2016). Modern society is fast-paced with high information flow, economic pressure, and rapid social change. Meditation can help bring about a more positive sense of self and is an essential part of the Eastern philosophical traditions addressed earlier within the scope of this book.

Breathing exercises are another option for improved stress management. Readers will know from experience that taking a few deep breaths can elicit a calming effect. Formalised and standardised breathing protocols can go further in improving one's well-being. Wim Hof, a Dutch man famous around the world for his record-setting ability to endure cold-exposure, has pioneered a now massively popular breathing technique for which instructional videos can be found via online search. Millions of people would not practice purposeful breathing without perceiving a benefit in their life. Beyond being legitimated by popular use, techniques such as Hof's have been found in clinical trials to increase happiness (Seppälä et al., 2020).

Meditation and purposeful breathing of the sort discussed can be performed independently as well as synergistically, such as in the practice of yoga. Yoga, stress, and happiness have been the subject of considerable study. The practice of yoga does not merely consist of striking particular poses. Yoga includes asana (holding poses), pranayama (adopting particular types of breathing), mindfulness and meditation exercises. As a result of combining these anti-stress practices, yoga has been found in clinical trials to increase happiness for individuals practicing it. One study in India, the birthplace of yoga, looked at happiness in a group of around 200 individuals practicing yoga compared to a control group and found that those who practiced yoga were happier (Gupta et al., 2016). Yoga has also been used and found as effective in the delivery of cognitive behavioral therapy in treating anxiety and improving happiness (Grensman et al., 2018).

Yoga, by and large, cannot be considered exercise as it does not sufficiently increase one's heart-rate. However, the association between yoga and happiness speaks to the broader established association between exercise and happiness. Exercise makes people happier. Happiness from a biological perspective results from the arrangement of particular chemicals in the body, namely dopamine, oxytocin, serotonin, endocannabinoids, endorphins, epinephrine, norepinephrine, cortisol, and melatonin (Dsouza et al., 2020). Exercise is effective at increasing and properly regulating these neurotransmitters. For tens of thousands of years, humans as a species have done hard labour and exercise to survive in relatively brutal environments. Today, our lifestyles of leisure and comfort and lack of physical activity may be making us less happy and fulfilled.

All this is to say that there are a variety of means by which it is possible to become happier through taking action to become less stressed. This short section does not purport to present readers with an exhaustive list of activities that tend to produce happiness. Indeed, these may vary significantly from person to person. The bottom line is that stress reduction is an essential part of finding and maintaining happiness.

**Gratitude**

Practicing gratitude is a free and easy method for enhancing one's level of happiness according to research. But what is gratitude exactly? Gratitude can be defined as "the appreciation of what is valuable and meaningful to oneself; it is a general state of thankfulness and/or appreciation" (Sansone & Sansone, 2010, p. 18). Gratitude of this type is an important skill to cultivate in our modern society where dissatisfaction runs rampant and is drilled into us by the forces of material culture. Dissatisfaction can arise from many sources, such as a perception of not having enough material goods or a large enough house compared to others (the age-old idea of keeping up with the Joneses). Dissatisfaction of this kind results most often as a consequence of society and social construction more than as a result of a genuine deprivation of some benefit held by others.

Gratitude can serve as a potent antidote to unwarranted feelings of dissatisfaction about one's place and position in life and thus leave you happier and more ready to enjoy the beauty of the world. Indeed, according to a study in 2008, gratitude uniquely predicts satisfaction with life and accounts for 20% of difference in individuals' level of life satisfaction (Wood et al., 2008). It appears that expressing gratitude more frequently and intensely is likely to make you happier. This does not mean forcing or feigning feelings of being grateful. Practicing gratitude can be simple. It can be as easy as appreciating and being thankful for a significant other, beautiful weather, or simply to awake feeling healthy on a given day. Readers will know from personal experience that spontaneous feelings of gratitude leave them feeling happier. To take gratitude one step further, research indicates that the key to promoting happiness may lie in making the conscious effort of becoming more grateful rather than just focusing on appreciating it where it arises.

Much like the phenomena of sleep and stress we just discussed, as well as the items addressed in the first chapter concerning objective elements of happiness, it is important to note that the connection between gratitude and happiness may have its roots in human evolutionary history. Gratitude and relationship with happiness may be in our DNA. It is plausible that gratitude and the happiness it brings emerged in evolution as a mechanism by which to increase the amount of reciprocal altruism happening among humans. For context, reciprocal altruism is when one individual performs a task for another at some cost to oneself for no immediate return, although there may be an unstated expectation for a future benefit. Studies on chimpanzee apes have established that chimps are more likely to help another member of their species if they had received help from that member in the past (Allen, 2018). This evidence indicates that there may be a broader evolutionary use of gratitude, which is that it enables greater social appreciation and collaboration. People who help each other are more successful than those who go at it alone and thus natural selection prefers cooperation in the form of reciprocal altruism.

In this way, gratitude as a practice to increase happiness links back to the previously addressed fact that social relationships that are meaningful are essential to a happy life. Gratitude as an emotion could also be said to fit into a larger frame of mind that is associated with happiness and well-being: positivity. Cultivating a sense of positivity can help ensure a greater degree of long-term happiness. A study in 2017 performed a longitudinal analysis of happiness and positivity among youth and found that a positive attitude and outlook on life significantly predicted happiness and success in a variety of domains of life such as workplace advancement (Caprara et al., 2017). It can be a useful mental exercise to look for the silver linings that exist in many unfortunate circumstances. However, a note of caution in this regard is advised. In summary, one way of leading a happier life is to quite literally count your blessings on a more regular and purposive basis.

## Purpose

The last century has seen the rise of existential thinking wherein people have questioned the purpose and value of the lives they lead. For most of human history, societies have been bound together based on shared faith to one sort of god or another. Certainly, in the western world, Christianity served as a powerful tool for social cohesion for many hundreds of years. The rise of modern rational thinking and widely held confidence in scientific knowledge and proof has led to the decline of religions, which in the past had given people meaning. As a result of the so-called death of God, some people today are concerned that their life and work has no inherent meaning or purpose (Roberts, 2007). This may be because, at least from a historical and rational account of life, it is true that humans are rapidly ageing organisms residing on a particular rock floating in space, most of whose lives have been forgotten in their entirety soon after death. This recognition of our own impending death and the weight of making choices in situations of unlimited variety can be the cause of unhappiness and regret. From a less philosophical standpoint, it may be true that some individuals are doing work that is legitimately meaningless in terms of serving some legitimate goal.

The book Bullshit Jobs: A Theory, by David Graeber argues that there is a significant portion of the labour market comprising jobs that are essentially unnecessary. This is problematic for peoples' happiness because there is nothing more "demoralizing than having to wake up in the morning five out of seven days of one's adult life to perform a task that one secretly believed did not need to be performed" (Fan, 2020, p. 1). The antidote to this feeling of meaningless is two-fold. First, it is important to find a way to earn a living that is meaningful. Second, it is important to take up activities that are meaningful.

On the first issue, evidence confirms that individuals that have meaningful jobs are happier than individuals who do not. This is shown in the fact that people would take significant salary reductions to have meaningful jobs. The Harvard Business Review found that American workers would on average give up "23% of their entire future lifetime earnings in order to have a job that was always meaningful" (Achor, 2018, para. 6). Forbes suggests several methods or finding meaningful work including (1) creating space in one's workflow and day to work on meaningful projects, (2) working with people who share similar goals, aspirations, and views as you do, (3) finding a job that involves helping/serving others in some manner, and (4) aligning your passions, values and gifts (eg. find a job that incorporates your hobby) (Castrillon, 2020). Finding meaningful work that pays well can be a long-term challenge. However, it can be a worthy goal in the end as happiness has the potential to result from meaningful work. Obviously, to be happy it is also important to have a job that pays reasonably, has sufficient and reasonable working hours, is not in a remote or unpleasant workplace, and has some sense of job security and stability, and is not highly stressful and highly difficult all the time.

Overall, there are several guiding principles that one can follow in choosing and building a meaningful career that will contribute to their happiness. We must not forget finding meaning outside the workplace, either. It is important to find meaning in adopting fulfilling hobbies like exercising, skiing, reading, painting, cooking, gardening, etc that involve interaction with the world and development of the self.

Another hobby that can lead to increases in happiness is volunteering for causes about which one is passionate. Evidence indicates that individuals that take up roles of voluntary service have the potential to improve mental health and be happier on average than individuals who are not involved in volunteerism (Ali et al., 2016). In fact, some studies addressing the value of volunteering go so far as to suggest that volunteering should be prescribed by doctors as a part of a wellness regime for the mental health benefits it offers participants (Johnson & Post, 2017).

Related to these ideas of finding meaning and volunteerism is the subject of charity. Here, too, there is the potential for people to become happier. Evidence suggests that engaging in acts of charity can lead to greater happiness. A study in 2020 showed that giving to someone in need not only offered an immediate benefit to the happiness of study participants, but that small acts of charity have the potential to aggregate into overall greater well-being (Aknin et al., 2020).

This chapter, and indeed much of this book, has focused on how people can live happier lives. It is important, however, to offer a word of caution in this regard. Research appears to indicate that individuals that are zealous about happiness promotion are unlikely to produce or achieve greater levels of happiness. Perhaps paradoxically, evidence indicates that people valuing happiness to an extreme degree are less likely to secure long term happiness (especially when they have low stress lives) and are more likely to have poor mental health compared to other individuals (Zerwas & Ford, 2021). The reason for the existence of this paradox could be that people who pursue happiness zealously may have unrealisable goals for happiness in mind, the non-fulfillment of which causes psychological stress. As the Taoist and Buddist philosophers from whom we heard earlier would point out, attachment and expectation are the roots of suffering. It appears safe to say, then, that pursuing happiness in all circumstances may not be realistic or an optimal means of operating in the world. Happiness is a complex, culturally-mediated, and individual phenomenon. Happiness promotion may be approached differently depending on the circumstances of an individual. People need to find and capture their own well-being, whether this involves adopting a particular theory of happiness or method for taking practical action to become happier.

Over the course of this book, we have taken a broad and holistic approach to the issue of happiness. It is intuitively clear that well-being is a foundational part of human existence and could be said to be the final goal each of us strives toward every day. We, as authors, have endeavored to offer readers a look into much which has been written about happiness over the long history of thought and reflection on the subject. We have attempted this by a variety of means. We have canvassed happiness as an emotional phenomenon. We have attempted to set out components of a theory of happiness. We have addressed, compared, and contrasted happiness as a concept seated in popular cultural and religious perspectives (ancient Greeks, Judeo-Christians, Taoists, Confucians, Buddhists, and Hindus). We have investigated the science of happiness as a subjective phenomenon and looked at the impact of society and interpersonal interaction on happiness. We have looked at the relationship between money and happiness as well as happiness from the view of psychological analysis. Finally, we have looked at research-backed practical methods that readers can adopt in their own lives as a potential means to becoming happier. All this is to say that the central purpose of this book as a whole was to offer readers context in the theory and practice of happiness. And we hope, at least by some small measure, the content of this book will enable readers to go forward purposefully in living lives of well-being.

# References

**Achor, S. (2018, November 6).** 9 Out of 10 People Are Willing to Earn Less Money to Do More-Meaningful Work. *Harvard Business Review.*

**Aknin, L. B., Dunn, E. W., Proulx, J., Lok, I., & Norton, M. I. (2020).** Does spending money on others promote happiness?: A registered replication report. Journal of Personality and *Social Psychology, 119*(2), e15.

**Ali, S. B., Khan, N. A., & Zehra, A. (2016).** Effect of Volunteerism on Mental Health and Happiness. *International Journal of Humanities and Social Sciences,* 123-130.

**Allen, S.** *The science of gratitude.* Greater Good Science Center at UC Berkeley John Templeton Foundation, 2018.

**Bartels, M. (2015).** Genetics of well-being and its components satisfaction with life, happiness, and quality of life: A review and meta-analysis of heritability studies. *Behaviour Genetics, 45*(2), 137-156.

**Baumeister, R. F., Bratslavsky, E., Finkenauer, C., & Vohs, K. D. (2001).** Bad is stronger than good. *Review of general psychology, 5*(4), 323-370.

**Berridge, Kent.** "The Debate over Dopamine's Role in Reward: The Case for Incentive Salience." Psychopharmacology 191:3 (2007): pp.391-431.

**Berridge, K. G., and M. L. Kringelbach.** "Affective Neuroscience of Pleasure: Reward in Humans and Animals." Psychopharmacology 199 (2008): pp.457-80,

**Boyd, R., & Richerson, P. J. (2009).** Culture and the evolution of human cooperation. *Philosophical Transactions of the Royal Society B: Biological Sciences, 364*(1533), pp. 3281-3288.

**Bruckner, D. W. (2016).** Quirky desires and well-being. *J. Ethics & Soc. Phil., 10,* p.1.

**Buckner, R. L., et al.** "The Brain's Default Network: Anatomy, Function, and Relevance to Disease." Annals of the New York Academy of Sciences 1124(2008): pp.1-38.

**Buddha And The Path To Happiness - An Overview (n.d.).** Pursuit of Happiness. Retrieved September 24, 2021 from https://www.pursuit-of-happiness.org/history-of-happiness/buddha/

**Campos, D., Cebolla, A., Quero, S., Bretón-López, J., Botella, C., Soler, J., ... & Baños, R. M. (2016).** Meditation and happiness: Mindfulness and self-compassion may mediate the meditation–happiness relationship. *Personality and individual differences, 93,* pp.80-85.

**Canada. (2021).** Ending long-term drinking water advisories. Indigenous Services Canada. Canada.ca. https://www.sac-isc.gc.ca/eng/1506514143353/1533317130660

**Capaldi, C. A., Dopko, R. L., & Zelenski, J. M. (2014).** The relationship between nature connectedness and happiness: A meta-analysis. *Frontiers in psychology, 5,* p.976.

**Carter, E. (2006).** Pre-packaged guided imagery for stress reduction: Initial results. *Counselling, Psychotherapy and Health, 2*(2), pp.27-39.

**Castrillon, C. (2020, July 28).** *5 strategies to find Meaningful work.* Forbes. Retrieved October 4, 2021, from https://www.forbes.com/sites/carolinecastrillon/2020/08/02/5-strategies-to-find-meaningful-work/.

**Chan, W. (1963).** *A source book in Chinese philosophy.* Princeton University Press.

**Chida, Y., & Steptoe, A. (2008).** Positive psychological well-being and mortality: a quantitative review of prospective observational studies. *Psychosomatic medicine, 70*(7), pp.741-756.

**Confucius and Happiness (n.d.).** Pursuit of Happiness. Retrieved September 24, 2021 from https://www.pursuit-of-happiness.org/history-of-happiness/confucius/

**Costanza, R., Hart, M., Kubiszewski, I., & Talberth, J. (2014).** A short history of GDP: Moving towards better measures of human well-being. Solutions, 5(1), 91-97.

**Damasio, A., & Carvalho, G. B. (2013).** The nature of feelings: evolutionary and neurobiological origins. *Nature reviews neuroscience, 14*(2), pp.143-152.

**De Vries, S., Nieuwenhuizen, W., Farjon, H., Van Hinsberg, A., & Dirkx, J. (2021).** In which natural environments are people happiest? Large-scale experience sampling in the Netherlands. *Landscape and urban planning, 205,* 103972.

**Demir, M., Özdemir, M., & Weitekamp, L. A. (2007).** Looking to happy tomorrows with friends: Best and close friendships as they predict happiness. *Journal of Happiness Studies, 8*(2), pp.243-271.

**Diener, E., & Lucas, R. E. (2000).** Explaining differences in societal levels of happiness: Relative standards, need fulfillment, culture, and evaluation theory. *Journal of Happiness Studies, 1*(1), 41-78.

**Diener, E., Seligman, M. (2004).** Beyond money. *Psychological Science in the Public Interest, 5*(1), 1–31. https://doi.org/10.1111/j.0963-7214.2004.00501001.x

**Diener, E. (2009).** *The science of well-being : the collected works of Ed Diener.* Springer Verlag.

**Diener, E. (2021).** Happiness: the science of subjective well-being. In R. Biswas-Diener & E. Diener (Eds), Noba textbook series: Psychology. Champaign, IL: DEF publishers. Retrieved from http://noba.to/qnw7g32t

**Drevets, W. C, et al.** "Subgenual Prefrontal Cortex Abnormalities in Mood Disorders." Nature 386:6627 (1997): pp.824-7.

**Dsouza, J., Chakraborty, A., & Veigas, J. (2020).** Biological Connection to the Feeling of Happiness. *Journal of Clinical & Diagnostic Research, 14*(10).

**Editors of Encyclopaedia Britannica, T. (2019, April 11).** *Tao-te-Ching.* Encyclopedia Britannica. https://www.britannica.com/topic/Tao-te-Ching

**ESRC. 2021.** The Easterlin Paradox. https://esrc.ukri.org/about-us/50-years-of-esrc/50-achievements/the-easterlin-paradox/

**Esteban Ortiz-Ospina and Max Roser (2013)** - "Happiness and Life Satisfaction". Published online at OurWorldInData.org. Retrieved from: 'https://ourworldindata.org/happiness-and-life-satisfaction' [Online Resource]

**Fan, Z. (2020).** Book Review: David Graeber, *Bullshit Jobs: A Theory.*

**Frede, D. (2017, December 21).** *Plato's ethics: An overview.* Stanford Encyclopedia of Philosophy. https://plato.stanford.edu/entries/plato-ethics/

**Freud, S., and J. Riviere.** Ci^nation and its Discontents. New York: J. Cape and H. Smith, 1930.

**Frijda, Nico.** "On the Nature and Function of Pleasure." Pleasures of the Brain. Eds. M. L. Kringelbach and K. C. Berridge. New York: Oxford University Press, 2010: pp.99-112.

**Giurge, L. M., Whillans, A. V., & West, C. (2020).** Why time poverty matters for individuals, organisations and nations. *Nature Human Behaviour, 4*(10), pp.993-1003.

**Goodwin, R. D., Weinberger, A. H., Kim, J. H., Wu, M., & Galea, S. (2020).** Trends in anxiety among adults in the United States, 2008–2018: Rapid increases among young adults. *Journal of psychiatric research, 130,* pp. 441-446.

**Grensman, A., Acharya, B. D., Wändell, P., Nilsson, G. H., Falkenberg, T., Sundin, Ö., & Werner, S. (2018).** Effect of traditional yoga, mindfulness–based cognitive therapy, and cognitive behavioral therapy, on health related quality of life: a randomized controlled trial on patients on sick leave because of burnout. *BMC complementary and alternative medicine, 18*(1), 1-16.

**Guo, T., & Hu, L. (2011).** Economic Determinants of Happiness. *arXiv preprint arXiv:1112.5802.*

**Gupta, R. K., Singh, S., & Singh, N. (2016).** Does yoga influence happiness and mental balance: A comparison between yoga practitioners and non-yoga practitioners. *OJMR, 2,* pp.1-5.

**Hall, J., & Helliwell, J. F. (2014).** Happiness and human development. *Occasional Paper, Human Development Report Office.*

**Haller, M., & Hadler, M. (2006).** How social relations and structures can produce happiness and unhappiness: An international comparative analysis. *Social indicators research, 75*(2), pp.169-216.

**Happiness, trust, and deaths under COVID-19 (2021, March 20).** World Happiness Report. https://worldhappiness.report/ed/2021/happiness-trust-and-deaths-under-covid-19/

**Haybron, D.** "Happiness", *The Stanford Encyclopedia of Philosophy* (Summer 2020 Edition), Edward N. Zalta (ed.).

**Hedonism (n.d.).** Merriam Webster. Retrieved September 20, 2021 from https://www.merriam-webster.com/dictionary/hedonism

**Hicks, D.** *Epicurus Letter to Menoeceus.* (2004). Massachusetts Institute of Technology.

**History.com Editors (2021, August 27).** *Hinduism.* History. Retrieved September 27, 2021 from https://www.history.com/topics/religion/hinduism

**Hou J., Walsh P., Zhang J. (2015)** The dynamics of Human Development Index, The Social Science Journal, 52:3, 331-347, DOI: 10.1016/j.soscij.2014.07.003

**Human Rights Watch (HRW).** 2016. Make it Safe. Canada's Obligation to end the First Nations Water Crisis. https://www.hrw.org/report/2016/06/07/make-it-safe/canadas-obligation-end-first-nations-water-crisis

**Johnson, S. S., & Post, S. G. (2017).** Rx It's good to be good (G2BG) 2017 commentary: Prescribing volunteerism for health, happiness, resilience, and longevity. *American Journal of Health Promotion.*

**Joshanloo, M. (2014).** Eastern conceptualizations of happiness: Fundamental differences with western views. *Journal of Happiness Studies, 15*(2), 475-493v. https://doi.org/10.1007/s10902-013-9431-1

Joshanloo, M., Lepshokova, Z. K., Panyusheva, T., Natalia, A., Poon, W., Yeung, V. W., Sundaram, S., Achoui, M., Asano, R., Igarashi, T., Tsukamoto, S., Rizwan, M., Khilji, I. A., Ferreira, M. C., Pang, J. S., Ho, L. S., Han, G., Bae, J., & Jiang, D. (2013). Cross-cultural validation of fear of happiness scale across 14 national groups. *Journal of Cross-Cultural Psychology, 45*(2), 246-264. https://doi.org/10.1177/0022022113505357

Joshanloo, M., & Weijers, D. (2014). Aversion to happiness across cultures: A review of where and why people are averse to happiness. *Journal of Happiness Studies, 15*(3), 717-735. https://doi.org/10.1007/s10902-013-9489-9

Kaiser Permanente. (2019). Stress management: Doing guided imagery to relax. Retrieved October 1, 2021, from https://wa.kaiserpermanente.org/kbase/topic.jhtml?docId=uz2270.

Kaltenmark, M., & Ames, R. T. (2020, February 5). *Laozi.* Encyclopedia Britannica. https://www.britannica.com/biography/Laozi

Killingsworth M.A. 2021. Experienced well-being rises with income, even above $75,000 per year. *Proceedings of the National Academy of Sciences. 118* (4) e2016976118; DOI: 10.1073/pnas.2016976118

Kim, E. S., Smith, J., & Kubzansky, L. D. (2014). Prospective study of the association between dispositional optimism and incident heart failure. *Circulation: Heart Failure, 7*(3), pp.394-400.

**Lamb, R., & Shields, J. (2021, September 1).** *How are fibonacci numbers expressed in nature?* HowStuffWorks Science. Retrieved October 4, 2021, from https://science.howstuffworks.com/math-concepts/fibonacci-nature.htm.

**Legatum Institute. 2020.** The Legatum Prosperity Index 2020. https://www.prosperity.com/feed/prosperity-index-tool-for-transformation

**Li, C., Wang, S., Zhao, Y., Kong, F., & Li, J. (2017).** The freedom to pursue happiness: Belief in free will predicts life satisfaction and positive affect among Chinese adolescents. *Frontiers in Psychology, 7,* 2027.

**Lopez, D. S. (2020, February 19).** *Buddha.* Encyclopedia Britannica. https://www.britannica.com/biography/Buddha-founder-of-Buddhism

**Luo, S. (2019).** Happiness and the good life: A classical Confucian perspective. *Dao, 18,* 41-58. https://doi.org/10.1007/s11712-018-9640-8

**Mark, J. J. (2020, July 9).** *Lao-Tzu.* World History Encyclopedia. Retrieved September 24, 2021 from https://www.worldhistory.org/Lao-Tzu/.

**MasterClass. (2021, January 27).** *Matthew Walker's 11 tips for improving sleep quality - 2021.* MasterClass. Retrieved October 1, 2021, from https://www.masterclass.com/articles/matthew-walker-on-improving-sleep-quality#why-is-sleep-important.

**Matz, S. C., Gladstone, J. J., & Stillwell, D. (2016).** Money buys happiness when spending fits our personality. *Psychological science, 27*(5), pp.715-725.

**McMahon, D. M. (2008).** The pursuit of happiness in history. The science of subjective well-being, 80-93.

**Michalos, A., Sharpe, A., Muhajarine, N. 2009.** An approach to a Canadian Index of Wellbeing. ResearchGate.

**Mill, J. S. (1859).** Utilitarianism (1863). *Utilitarianism, Liberty, Representative Government,* pp.7-9.

**Moore, C. (2021, March 5).** *What is eudaimonia? Aristotle and eudaimonic well-being.* Positive Psychology. https://positivepsychology.com/eudaimonia/

**National Geographic Society (2020a, August 19).** *Confucianism.* National Geographic. Retrieved September 26, 2021 from https://www.nationalgeographic.org/encyclopedia/confucianism/

**National Geographic Society (2020b, August 31).** *Taoism.* National Geographic. Retrieved September 26, 2021 from https://www.nationalgeographic.org/encyclopedia/taoism/

**Nishpapananda, S. (2010).** Hinduism, happiness, and the good life. *Interdisciplinary Journal of the Dedicated Semester, 1,* Article 11. Retrieved from https://griffinshare.fontbonne.edu/ijds/vol1/iss1/11

**Nozick, R., & Williams, B. (2014).** *Anarchy, State and Utopia.* Princeton University Press.

**Oishi, S., Graham, J., Kesebir, S., & Galinha, I. C. (2013).** Concepts of happiness across time and cultures. *Personality and Social Psychology Bulletin, 39*(5), 559-577. https://doi.org/10.1177/0146167213480042

**Ott, J. (2005).** Level and Inequality of Happiness in Nations: Does Greater Happiness of a Greater Number Imply Greater Inequality in Happiness? *Journal of Happiness Studies, 6*(4), 397–420. https://doi.org/10.1007/s10902-005-8856-6

**Pouw, N., & McGregor, A. (2014).** An Economics of Wellbeing: What would economics look like if it were focused on human well-being?. IDS Working Papers, 2014(436), 1-27.

**Quinn, P. C., Kelly, D. J., Lee, K., Pascalis, O., & Slater, A. M. (2008).** Preference for attractive faces in human infants extends beyond conspecifics. *Developmental science, 11*(1), 76-83.

**Radford, T. (2004, September 6).** *How beauty fascinates from birth.* The Guardian. Retrieved October 1, 2021, from https://www.theguardian.com/science/2004/sep/06science.research2.

**Rahman, A. A., & Veenhoven, R. (2018).** Freedom and happiness in nations: A research synthesis. *Applied Research in Quality of Life, 13*(2), pp.435-456.

**Ricard, M. (2014).** A Buddhist view of happiness. *Journal of Law and Religion, 29*(1), pp.14-29. https://doi.org/10.1017/jlr.2013.9

**Roberts, M. (2007).** Modernity, mental illness and the crisis of meaning. *Journal of Psychiatric and Mental Health Nursing, 14*(3), pp.277-281.

**Røysamb, E., Nes, R.B., Czajkowski, N.O., Vassend, O. 2018.** Genetics, personality and wellbeing. A twin study of traits, facets and life satisfaction. Sci Rep 8, 12298. https://doi.org/10.1038/s41598-018-29881-x

**Rojas, M. 2019.** The Economics of Happiness: How the Easterlin Paradox Transformed Our Understanding of Well-Being and Progress. https://doi.org/10.1007/978-3-030-15835-4

**Ruberton, P. M., Gladstone, J., & Lyubomirsky, S. (2016).** How your bank balance buys happiness: The importance of "cash on hand" to life satisfaction. *Emotion, 16*(5), p.575.

**Saghir, Z., Syeda, J. N., Muhammad, A. S., & Abdalla, T. H. B. (2018).** The amygdala, sleep debt, sleep deprivation, and the emotion of anger: a possible connection?. *Cureus, 10*(7).

**Sansone, R. A., & Sansone, L. A. (2010).** Gratitude and well being: The benefits of appreciation. *Psychiatry (Edgmont), 7*(11), p.18.

**Sapranaviciute-Zabazlajeva, L., Luksiene, D., Virviciute, D., Bobak, M., & Tamosiunas, A. (2017).** Link between healthy lifestyle and psychological well-being in Lithuanian adults aged 45–72: a cross-sectional study. *BMJ open, 7*(4), e014240.

**Sartorius, N. (2006).** The meanings of health and its promotion. *Croatian medical journal, 47*(4), p.662.

**Sartwell, C,** "Beauty", The Stanford Encyclopedia of Philosophy (Winter 2017 Edition), Edward N. Zalta (ed.).

**Schiffrin, H. H., & Nelson, S. K. (2010).** Stressed and happy? Investigating the relationship between happiness and perceived stress. *Journal of happiness studies, 11*(1), pp.33-39.

**Seligman, M. F., et al.** "Positive Psychology Progress: Empirical Validation of Interventions." American Psychologist 60:5 (2005): pp.410-21.

**Seligman, M. F., et al.** "Flourish" (2012): pp.1-53.

**Seresinhe, C. I., Preis, T., MacKerron, G., & Moat, H. S. (2019).** Happiness is greater in more scenic locations. *Scientific Reports, 9*(1), pp.1-11.

**Shin, J. E., & Kim, J. K. (2018).** How a good sleep predicts life satisfaction: the role of zero-sum beliefs about happiness. *Frontiers in psychology, 9,* 1589.

**Seppälä, E. M., Bradley, C., Moeller, J., Harouni, L., Nandamudi, D., & Brackett, M. A. (2020).** Promoting mental health and psychological thriving in university students: a randomized controlled trial of three well-being interventions. *Frontiers in psychiatry, 11,* p.590.

**Snyder, C. R., Lopez, S. J., Pedrotti, J. T. (2010).** *Positive psychology: The scientific and practical explorations of human strengths* (2nd ed.). SAGE Publications.

**Statistics Canada. 2021.** National Gross Domestic Product by Income and by Expenditure Accounts. https://www23.statcan.gc.ca/imdb/p2SV.pl?Function=getSurvey&SDDS=1901

**Stearns, P. N. (2012).** The history of happiness. *Harvard business review, 90*(1-2), 104-109.

**Steve Derne. (2016).** Sociology of Well-being and Aeing: Lessons From India. Sage Publications Pvt. Ltd.

**Sun, J., Harris, K., & Vazire, S. (2019).** Is well-being associated with the quantity and quality of social interactions?. *Journal of Personality and Social Psychology.*

**Thomas Aquinas (n.d.).** Pursuit of Happiness. Retrieved September 9, 2021 from https://www.pursuit-of-happiness.org/history-of-happiness/thomas-aquinas/

**Twenge, J. M., & Cooper, A. B. (2020).** The expanding class divide in happiness in the United States, 1972–2016. *Emotion.*

**Van Buitenen, J. A. B., Doniger, W., Gold, A. G., Narayanan, V., Dimock, E. C., Smith, B. K., &   Basham, A. L. (2020, November 30).** *Hinduism.* Encyclopedia Britannica. https://www.britannica.com/topic/Hinduism

**Veenhoven, R. (2000).** Freedom and happiness: A comparative study in forty-four nations in the early 1990s. Culture and subjective well-being, pp.257-288.

**Veenhoven, R. (2008).** Sociological theories of Subjective Well-Being.  The science of subjective well-being. Guilford Press.(p. 44)

**Veenhoven, R. (2008).** How do we assess how happy we are? Tenets, implications and tenability of three theories. Erasmus University Rotterdam, Netherlands

**Veenhoven, R. (2014).** Sociology's Blind Eye For Happiness. Comparative Sociology 13. P 537-555. DOI 10.1163/15691330-12341324. Brill Academic Publishers

**Veenhoven R. (2019)** Happiness in Canada (CA), Erasmus University Rotterdam, The Netherlands.World Database of Happiness

**WDH. (n.d.).** World database of happiness: archive of research findings on subjective enjoyment of life. World Database of Happiness. Retrieved September 9, 2021, from https://worlddatabaseofhappiness.eur.nl/this-database/glossary/.

Weiming, T. (2019, August 12). *Confucianism.* Encyclopedia Britannica. https://www.britannica.com/topic/Confucianism

**White, M., & Foulds, F. (2018).** Symmetry is its own reward: on the character and significance of Acheulean handaxe symmetry in the Middle Pleistocene. *antiquity, 92*(362), pp.304-319.

**Wierzbicka, A. (2004).** "Happiness" in cross-linguistic & crosscultural perspective. *Daedalus, 133,* pp.34-43. https://www.jstor.org/stable/20027911

**Wood, A. M., Joseph, S., & Maltby, J. (2008).** Gratitude uniquely predicts satisfaction with life: Incremental validity above the domains and facets of the five factor model. *Personality and individual differences, 45*(1), pp.49-54.

**World Happiness Report FAQ (n.d.).** Retrieved October 2, 2021 from https://worldhappiness.report/faq/

**Yang L. (2018)** Measuring Well-being: A Multidimensional Index Integrating Subjective Well-being and Preferences, Journal of Human Development and Capabilities, 19:4, pp.456-476, DOI: 10.1080/19452829.2018.1474859.

**Zerwas, F. K., & Ford, B. Q. (2021).** The paradox of pursuing happiness. *Current Opinion in Behavioral Sciences, 39*, pp.106-112.

www.ingramcontent.com/pod-product-compliance
Lightning Source LLC
Chambersburg PA
CBHW051943160426
43198CB00013B/2283